HMS
Detroit

THE
BATTLE
FOR
LAKE ERIE

HMS Detroit
THE BATTLE FOR LAKE ERIE

Robert Malcomson
Thomas Malcomson

NAVAL INSTITUTE PRESS
Annapolis, Maryland

First published in Canada in 1990 by
Vanwell Publishing Limited
1 Northrup Cresent, Box 2131
St. Catharines, Ontario
L2M 6P5

Design Susan Nicholson
Maps Loris Gasparotto

Published and distributed in the
United States of America
by the Naval Institute Press, Annapolis,
Maryland 21402

Library of Congress Catalog No.
90–63199

ISBN 1–55750–053–3

Printed and bound in Canada by T.H. Best
Printing Company Limited, Don Mills,
Ontario.

CONTENTS

Acknowledgements vii

Introduction ix

Chapter 1
THE WAR ALONG THE LAKES 11

Chapter 2
ROBERT BARCLAY, R. N. 20

Chapter 3
FROM KINGSTON TO LAKE ERIE 29

Chapter 4
OLIVER HAZARD PERRY, U. S. N. 42

Chapter 5
PROBLEMS AT AMHERSTBURG 53

Chapter 6
THE FAILED BLOCKADE 64

Chapter 7
THE COMPLAINTS OF AUGUST 73

Chapter 8
WAR COUNCILS 84

Chapter 9
THE BATTLE 94

Chapter 10
"THIS VICTORY SO DECISIVE AND IMPORTANT" 112

Chapter 11
MEN AND SHIPS 121

Chapter Notes 131

Bibliography 143

This book is dedicated to
our father
Alfred Malcomson (1917-1980)
who introduced us
to the age of fighting sail
when we were little boys.

ACKNOWLEDGMENTS

There would be no book if we had not received the unfailing support and encouragement of the ones who are closest to us in our lives, so our thanks go first to Janet and Peggy, Max and Melanie and Carrie. Thanks also to moms, Nancy Jenner and Jenny Malcomson, who never tire of hearing about what we're doing.

Timothy Dubé from the National Archives in Ottawa, Sheridan Alder and David Webb of Fort Malden Historic Park in Amherstburg were of great assistance by providing copies of period documents from their collections. Keith Aiken and Gordon Skinner provided important details concerning the hand weapons and uniforms of the War of 1812. A note of thanks is offered to the staff of the Baldwin Room and Ross Robertson Collection at the Metro Toronto Reference Library for their work with the authors in discovering important articles and pictures of the people and places involved in our story. We would like to thank the Royal Canadian Military Institute, Toronto, for allowing us to access its members-only library. The Special Collections room at the Brock University library provided many of the documentary material used during the research of the book.

Thanks to John Claridge, editor of *The Journal of Erie Studies*, for making available the picture collection of the Erie Historical Society. Also, appreciation is extended to Donald K. Beman of Beman Galleries for giving us access to the Julian Davidson painting of the battle. Similarly, the Buffalo Historical Society made various pieces of art work available. The paintings by Peter Rindlisbacher were of great value during our research and discussions about the ships and the battle.

John H. Adams conducted a search on behalf of the authors in the Public Records Office in London, England, and uncovered biographical information regarding Robert Barclay.

To the members of Project HMS Detroit, Zane Handysides, Hy Shenker, Dr. Paul Smith and John James who provided information concerning the efforts to build a new *Detroit*, we extend our appreciation. A special acknowledgment is offered to Murray Kennedy, chair of the Project HMS Detroit committee, for his encouragement to write this book. Mayor William Gibb and past mayor Garnet Fox of Amherstburg and town clerk Tom Killgalin were of great assistance to us during our visits in Amherstburg.

Draft copies of the manuscript were read by Fred Drake and Barry Gough. Their comments regarding the material and its treatment were of significant value to us as we polished the text.

Lastly, we owe gratitude to Vanwell Publishing for having faith in our project and making it possible to bring this tale to print.

Forming the foundation for the first reconstruction of the *Niagara*, the brig's original hull and keel lay on the shore of Erie harbour after being raised from the mud of Misery Bay on April 2, 1913.

INTRODUCTION

This book began with a visit to Erie, Pennsylvania, on September 10, 1988 for the 175th anniversary of the battle of Lake Erie. The day's celebrations saw thousands of people crowd the harbour to view the launch of the reconstructed US Brig *Niagara*. We had front row seats at that event and even managed to wangle our way on board the vessel while it still rested high and dry on its transportable cradle. The hull was beautiful, so graceful and perfect. Its broad planking was freshly painted in black and muted green. Chest-high bulwarks glistened like gold, pierced with the bright red mouths of gun ports. Two flags flapped and cracked in the breeze; Perry's "Don't Give Up the Ship" at the bow, the Stars and Stripes above the stern. As the keel kissed the waters of Erie Harbour, the onlookers responded with a great ovation.

The launch of the *Niagara* was a sparkling example of the dedication that the people of Pennsylvania have shown toward preserving their past. Into the rebuilt brig were fitted pieces of wood from the original warship that bore Oliver Hazard Perry's flag at the moment of his victory on that sunny September Friday in 1813. The first *Niagara* was retired from duty in 1818 and scuttled along with other ships from the battle in Misery Bay at Erie. It was raised in 1913 and restored for a centennial celebration, after which neglect and time reduced it to a derelict. During the 1930s the Pennsylvania Historical and Museum Commission took responsibility for the *Niagara* and over the next fifty years it evolved through a series of incomplete refits, until the latest restoration project began. After its launch at Erie in 1988, the brig was powered out into the bay by a tugboat to join the fleet of pleasure craft in a procession along the shoreline. Despite its lack of masts and "furniture," it was impossible to see that wooden ship without picturing how it must have looked, armed and cruising the waters west of Put-in-Bay. Like magic, the ship brought history back to life.

Before leaving Erie that day, we went looking for the story of the *Niagara* and the men who fought it. We found a couple of slim volumes and a collector's piece, each of them refreshing our memory of how Perry earned glory with his capture of an entire British squadron. It was in a copy of the special edition of the *Journal of Erie Studies*, however, that we made the discovery that led to this book. A simple paragraph on the editor's page made reference to the HMS *Detroit* Project, an undertaking by a group of Canadians to build the opposite number of the *Niagara*.

Early in the 1980s a group of people from the Amherstburg, Ontario area decided to recreate the corvette HMS *Detroit*, flagship of the British squadron. A decade of patient, but deliberate planning has brought the *Detroit* Project close to its objective. As this book goes to press, the actual construction of the ship awaits funding. It was the enthusiasm of the Amherstburg group's effort that motivated us to investigate the story of the battle of Lake Erie.

Our early research quickly revealed the basics of the tale. The battle of Lake Erie was a spectacular event, but it did not occur in a vacuum. It was, instead, the explosion that came at the end of a long string of events, some of them occurring months and many kilometres apart, but all of them intermeshed into the chaos that is war. To understand why things turned out as they did on the waters west of Put-in-Bay requires a close look at how the fight for control of Lake Ontario affected the Lake Erie theatre, at how the American supply train underlay Perry's success, at how military command decisions determined the effectiveness of naval operations.

The battle itself had some unique qualities. Unusual indeed was such a total defeat for a British squadron during the early 1800s. Never before or since has a clash of such proportions occurred on the peaceful waters of the Great Lakes. Out of the stunning American victory came a poisonous quarrel between its heroes, one that is still being argued today. On the other hand, the beaten commander went before a court martial, having lost an entire squadron, and walked away exonerated.

When the cannonade ended and the question of control was settled, the survivors and their ships did not cease to exist. The schooners and brigs and corvettes, upon which so much of the struggle had balanced, continued to ply the lakes, some of them coming to firey ends, others fated for unexpected outcomes. The men went to prison and the beach and careers of brief renown or considerable longevity.

Looking into the many accounts of the battle of Lake Erie also revealed that precious little has been written about the men who sailed HMS *Detroit* and its sister ships away from Amherstburg to challenge the American squadron. From the earliest narratives the emphasis has been on Perry's exertions to build his ships and to gain supremacy of Lake Erie. His contemporaries, among them Usher Parsons, Daniel Dobbins and Jesse Elliott, survived to recount their versions of what happened during the summer of 1813. Writers like Benson Lossing and James Fenimore Cooper detailed the events as they unfolded before, during and after the battle, but with the American camp most sharply in focus. In a similar manner, Mahan and Roosevelt described the episode, giving much attention to tactics, but very little to the men in the British ships. When the centennial of the victory came around, the *Niagara* was resurrected and an impressive tower was built at Put-in-Bay to honour Perry's success. Scarce were the words about the men who had lost the day and given their blood for a cause they held just as dearly as the one for which Perry fought. The names of three British officers buried beneath Perry's column are not even recorded there.

The idea that a re-creation of HMS *Detroit* might be moored at Amherstburg someday guided our research beyond the classic telling of the battle and illuminated more clearly the situation as it existed on the British side of the water. Articles written by Buckie and Drake, Stacey and Douglas steered us in the right direction. The documentaries of Cruikshank and Wood, combined with an assortment of unpublished material, presented us with the evidence needed to assemble the cast who played out their roles for king and country. Slowly the ghostly figure of Commander Robert Barclay, R. N. came alive. Out of the shadows stepped men who also experienced the desperate circumstances on the Lake Erie front. The weaknesses in the supply line and the frustrations in the chain of command became apparent. Missed opportunities, faulty decisions and the seemingly biased hand of fate wove themselves into the circumstances that led to the British defeat.

The outcome of our research has been to present a balanced account of the men, the ships and the events involved in the battle of Lake Erie. It is our aspiration that the reader will come away from this book with a broader understanding of that episode. Our treatment of the story aims to give the brig *Niagara* its rightful place of honour without forgetting the dignity owing to His Majesty's Ship *Detroit*.

Robert Malcomson, St. Catharines

Thomas Malcomson, North York, 1990

1
THE WAR ALONG THE LAKES

JUST BEFORE NOON on September 10, 1813, an iron ball fired from the deck of HMS *Detroit* sliced through the water rippling ahead of the U.S. Brig *Lawrence* and disappeared. It was followed minutes later by a second ranging shot. This one found its mark, crashing through the bulwarks in the bow of the *Lawrence* and sending a hail of jagged splinters across the forecastle of the brig. With that first direct hit, British Commander Robert Heriot Barclay signalled the beginning of the climactic battle for supremacy of Lake Erie. For the next three hours the violent struggle between his squadron and that of Oliver Hazard Perry evolved into the single most calamitous confrontation to ever take place on the Great Lakes. To the victor would go the much sought-after prize: control of the waterway that bridged British and American territories. For Perry and Barclay, upon whose shoulders the expectations of their separate nations weighed heavily, the events of that afternoon held the promise of fame and the ignominy of defeat. After months of wary surveillance of each other's naval forces, the two young commanders bravely faced the question of control of the lake head-on.

The fuses that sparked the opening shots of the battle of Lake Erie were long indeed. They stretched back in time over more than a year of formal conflict between the United States and Britain. President James Madison had declared war against Britain on June 18, 1812, causing the war hawks in the American Congress to rejoice at having finally obtained the power to strike back at the British. No more would they have to watch passively while the Royal Navy, without any regard for the fledgling American sovereignty, took sailors from American merchant ships on the high seas or, by their blockade of French

11

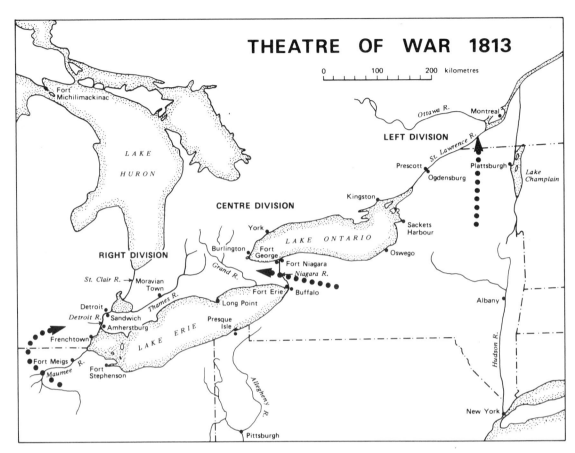

THEATRE OF WAR 1813

The inland theatre of war at the outbreak of hostilities. An easy march to victory was anticipated by the war hawks in the American Congress. Three points of invasion were predicted to bring about a quick surrender of the British forces.

ports, prevented free trade with Europe. At last, decisive action could be taken on the western frontier against the tribes of Indians who had been supplied for years by the British. Eager for a fight, the small but potent American navy prepared for sea, its guns primed for combat. The military commanders formed up their rank and file and fixed their sights on the vulnerable provinces of Upper and Lower Canada. With the main strength of the British army focused on impeding Napoleon's conquest of Europe, those provinces seemed like easy pickings.

A three-pronged invasion plan was developed by the Americans during that first summer of the 1812 war. It seemed simple enough to send armies to attack the British settlements along the Detroit River, the Niagara River and near Montreal. Once having occupied those British centres, it would be possible to march around the northern shores of the lakes and down the St. Lawrence River to British headquarters at Quebec. Within a few weeks the provinces would undoubtedly yield. Just like in the glorious days of the revolutionary war (1776-1783), Britain would fall to its knees in humiliation.

The road to victory did not materialize so easily. The army designated to travel from

Prior to the onset of the 1812 war, George Prevost (1767-1816) quelled threats of rebellion in Lower Canada, by including French Canadians in the administration of the province.

Lake Champlain towards Montreal bogged down far short of its target. General William Hull successfully crossed the Detroit River with his forces in July of 1812, but soon withdrew timidly to Fort Detroit. Weeks later he surrendered the fort and his men to Major General Isaac Brock and the Indian allies under their great leader, Tecumseh. Major General Stephen Van Rensselaer held the beachhead at Queenston for a few hours in October until British regiments, rallying to avenge their fallen General Brock, captured most of his troops. The easy conquest of Canada quickly ground to a halt.

The defense of the Canadian provinces had been managed by the thinnest of red lines. British settlements were scattered along the lakeshores and rivers from Quebec to the Island of Michilimackinac on Lake Huron and beyond. The territory was divided into zones of defense, war fronts where the Americans crossed the border or planned to. The Left Division was closest to the headquarters at Quebec and included the St. Lawrence River up to Kingston. The Centre Division enclosed Niagara and York, and the area west of Lake Erie became known as the Right Division. Fortresses had been built at places like Montreal, Kingston, York, Niagara and Amherstburg, but the muster rolls at most of these garrisons showed that only scant hundreds of soldiers could be called upon in each place to oppose the invading Americans.

In charge of defending the border was Sir George Prevost, governor general and commander in chief of the King's forces, not only in Upper and Lower Canada, but in the Atlantic provinces and Bermuda as well. Prevost, born in 1767, had begun his military career at the age of twelve by joining his father's regiment. His family's wealth helped to secure him the rank of major by 1790. Diplomacy became the centre of Prevost's career as he moved through a number of minor governorships before being assigned in 1811 to the post of governor general at Quebec. His fluency with French made him a perfect choice for the position, but the American declaration of war presented him with a burdensome tangle of problems that required more than just diplomatic expertise.

Prior to 1812 Isaac Chauncey's (1776-1841) experience included service as an officer in America's wars with France and Tripoli at the turn of the century. When war was declared, he was commandant of the New York Navy Yard.

With over a thousand kilometres of border to protect, Prevost's task was monumental. To preserve the provinces, he needed talented and resourceful subordinate officers, like Isaac Brock whose death at the battle of Queenston Heights was a significant setback. Brock's skill and decisiveness as a leader, combined with the fighting strength of the well-disciplined regulars, would have been a great asset in the efforts to defend the provinces. The men who held command immediately after Brock seldom lived up to his example. Sir Roger Hale Sheaffe, who took over Brock's post as commander in chief and administrator for the province of Upper Canada, was unpopular and eventually replaced by Major General Francis Baron De Rottenburg who lacked Brock's concern for the western reaches of the province. Even Prevost himself, a career diplomat, was hardly cut out for the role that called for a hard-nosed and determined captain general.

Selecting officers to oversee the various far-flung outposts was only one of Prevost's problems. None of those garrisons could survive for long without a continuous flow of supplies, since everything they needed, from muskets to mortars, from tunics to rum, had to be transported across the vast Canadian wilderness. To make matters more difficult, the British provinces lacked the industrial resources to produce the required armaments and provisions. As a result, such materiel had to be imported from England, where the fight against Napoleon continued to monopolize the mother country's supply network. For Sir George Prevost, the War of 1812 became a matter of stretching men and munitions to the limit, while he strove to keep the wolf from the door.

Despite the complexities of Governor General Prevost's management problems, a stiff enough opposition was presented in 1812 to forestall the American wolf. Late in the summer of that year it became obvious to President Madison's war cabinet that a conquest of the provinces was going to require a greater investment in time and energy. Accordingly, by the end of the year the Army of the Northwest, numbering more than five thousand and led by Brigadier General William Henry Harrison, set off through harsh winter weather for the Detroit region. Major General Henry Dearborn was given the command of the refortified Army of the Centre, while the third army north of Lake Champlain was likewise reinforced.

The escalation in the American war effort also saw an expansion in the role of the navy. If large armies were going to be on the move and full-scale assaults were going to be made on well-defended positions, dependable supply routes had to be kept open. In 1812 there were few roads cut through the countryside of the northern states that were suitable for the task at hand. The best routes for meeting the transportation needs of armies were the waterways. This point was one that A. T. Mahan made in his *Sea Power In Its Relation To The War Of 1812.* "The importance of the lakes to military operations must always be great," Mahan wrote, "but it was much enhanced in 1812 by the undeveloped condition of land communications. From Lake Superior to the head of the first rapid of the St. Lawrence, therefore, the control of the water was the decisive factor in the general military situation."[1]

Madison and his advisors came to realize that control of Lake Ontario and Lake Erie would provide the foundation upon which their revised invasion efforts could be built. As a result, plans were laid for a naval build-up on the Great Lakes aimed at attaining the supremacy necessary for keeping the supply lines open.

Captain Isaac Chauncey was administering the naval yard at New York when the request arrived for him to report to Washington. He was forty-one years old, a veteran with service in warships and the merchant marine. Secretary of the Navy Paul Hamilton ordered Chauncey to assemble and man squadrons that would make the Americans the masters of the inland seas. By the end of September 1812, Chauncey had already sent tonnes of materiel and hundreds of sailors and labourers to Sackets Harbour, the naval base in the eastern corner of Lake Ontario.[2]

Prior to the war the American naval presence on the Great Lakes was minimal, to say the least. On Lake Erie, a one-armed vessel, the 6-gun brig *Adams*, had flown the Stars and Stripes until it was hauled down after General Hull's surrender of Detroit in August. Another brig, the *Oneida* carrying sixteen cannons, was the only American warship on Lake Ontario. Its commander, Lieutenant Melancthon Woolsey, quickly purchased American merchant schooners for conversion into fighting ships. It was this sparse naval force that Isaac Chauncey inherited at Sackets Harbour during the fall of 1812. He set to work outfitting a squadron to cruise the lake, while also laying down the keel for a proper warship and making plans for future constructions.

Simultaneously, Chauncey oversaw, albeit at some distance, a parallel build-up on Lake Erie where two projects were already underway. In September Navy Secretary Paul Hamilton had ordered Daniel Dobbins, a master mariner from the upper lakes, to undertake the construction of gunboats at Presque Isle, Pennsylvania.[3] About the same time, naval Lieutenant Jesse Elliott began collecting schooners at Black Rock near the settlement of Buffalo. To add to the Black Rock vessels, Elliott, in a demonstration of his professional zeal, captured from under the noses of the British at Fort Erie two of their armed vessels. He was only successful in bringing one of them, the brig *Caledonia*, over to the American side. The second ship, the former *Adams*, renamed *Detroit* in honour of Brock's victory, was wrecked during an attempt by the British to reclaim it.[4]

Capture of the *Lord Nelson*. On June 5, 1812 the brig *Oneida*, launched in 1809 and operating as a revenue cutter patrolling Lake Ontario, captured the British schooner on suspicion of smuggling. Lieutenant Woolsey, in command of the *Oneida*, purchased the schooner for service in the navy. It was renamed the *Scourge* and armed with ten guns.

Sir George Prevost was also keenly aware of the importance the lakes would play in maintaining the strength of the British line of defense. Unlike his American counterparts, however, he did have a naval force already in place. During the French and Indian War (1754-1763), Britain had established an armed presence on the North American lakes, which was revived and reorganized during the American revolutionary war. In 1785 the "lake navy" was placed under the control of the military establishment at Quebec and eventually became known as the Provincial Marine. At the beginning of the 1812 war some of the officers and men in the marine had roots in the Royal Navy, but the organization was autonomous of the navy, being essentially a floating arm of the military. The ships in the squadrons on Lake Ontario and the upper lakes were maintained for conducting government business and for transporting troops when that need arose. As bases for the Provincial Marine, naval establishments had been set up where shipbuilding could be conducted and supplies warehoused. In 1812 the key naval establishments were at Kingston and Amherstburg, while there was a small yard at Quebec.

At the outbreak of war, the Provincial Marine was barely able to meet the threat of the American invasion, since no concentrated effort had been made over the years to keep the squadrons in the condition necessary for fighting a war. A report dealing with the proposed organization for the marine for the year 1812 revealed, for instance, that three small vessels were being manned on Lake Ontario and only two on Lake Erie. Plans had been made to build another schooner on each lake, but even that meagre increment would strain the army's efforts to provide crews, since there were fewer than one hundred seamen on the payroll. To command those men, who were often referred to with some derision as "Canadians", there were two commanders and seven lieutenants and mates. Similarly, at the three shipyards only two master builders, two foremen and one blacksmith were employed.[5] A later tally, completed in March of 1813, showed that the situation, after almost a year of war, had barely improved. It was estimated that a further 450 men were required, if the existing ships and three more under construction would be even marginally manned.[6]

Not only was the Provincial Marine sparsely staffed at the outbreak of hostilities with the United States, but a number of its officers were considered incompetent. Captain Andrew Gray, acting deputy quarter master general and the watchdog on the state of the marine, minced no words when he summarized his views on the conditions of the Lake Ontario squadron in a report sent to Sir George Prevost on December 3, 1812:

> The officers of the Marine appear to be destitute of all energy and spirit, and are sunk into contempt in the eyes of all who know them. The want of seamen is so great that the *Royal George* has only 17 men on board who are capable of doing their Duty, and the *Moira* only 10 able seamen. On the other hand the efforts of the enemy are such, that nothing can save our Navy from destruction, the moment the navigation opens in the spring.[7]

The British had been able to maintain a presence on the lakes over the years, but that force was poorly suited to handle the job of maintaining supremacy of the waterways. Even before Gray expressed his dismay to Governor General Prevost, the Americans had demonstrated their growing strength at the expense of the Provincial Marine. In November 1812 Commodore Chauncey, with his makeshift fleet, had harrassed the Lake Ontario squadron

The *Royal George* being pursued by the American Lake Ontario squadron, November 8-10, 1812. Commodore Chauncey reported, "The *Royal George* must have received very considerable injury in her hull and men, as the gun vessels with a long 32-pounder were seen to strike her almost every shot . . . The *Royal George* was driven into the inner harbour . . . by the *Oneida* and four small schooners."

and chased it into Kingston harbour with its tail between its legs, causing Chauncey to claim supremacy as ice conditions ended the navigation season.[8]

Prevost understood the inadequacies of the Provincial Marine and knew that the only hope for counteracting the growth of the American squadrons was "tried officers . . . and trusty men from the Navy."[9] With that idea in mind, he wrote to Lord Bathurst, the colonial secretary of the Tory government in England, and to Sir John Borlase Warren, who from his headquarters at Halifax commanded naval operations in the waters between Newfoundland and the West Indies. From those men he requested that contingents of experienced seamen be sent to the lakes, so that Prevost could use them to secure the waterways and thereby keep his military forces successfully in the field.

Riding the crest of his early success against the Provincial Marine, Isaac Chauncey was also looking for ambitious officers and crews to man the squadrons he planned to create on the lakes during the season of 1813. There was no doubt that control of the Great Lakes would be a prerequisite to victory in the land war.

Out of the need to gain mastery of the waterways evolved the events that led to the battle for Lake Erie. During the spring of 1813, two young naval officers arrived on the lakes to take on key roles in that struggle. Robert Heriot Barclay, a lieutenant aboard one of His Majesty's frigates on the North American station, was recalled to Halifax and sent inland. His eventual adversary, Oliver Hazard Perry, in charge of a flotilla of gunboats near Newport, Rhode Island, received orders to place himself under Isaac Chauncey's supervision. Before the following summer was over, these two men had sailed their squadrons into battle and played their parts in the critical competition for naval supremacy.

2

ROBERT BARCLAY, R. N.

ROBERT HERIOT BARCLAY came to the Great Lakes war a tried and true seaman, cut in the pattern of the ideal British naval officer. For more than half his life he had served King George III and proudly bore the scars of that service. His appointment to the lakes was a promotion he had long awaited and meant that he would at last get the chance to demonstrate his worth in an independent command.

Barclay came from Scottish stock.[1] He was born at the manse in King's Kettle, Fife, on September 18, 1785, the second son of Reverend Peter Barclay and Margaret Duddingstone. With his two brothers he attended a local school where John Strachan, a man whose destiny also lay in Upper Canada, held classes.

Young Robert's formal education came to an early end when his parents were able to find a position for him in the Royal Navy. It was the influence of his uncle, Admiral William Duddingstone, that secured the twelve-year-old boy a place in the midshipmen's berth of the 44-gun frigate *Anson*, commanded by Captain Philip Durham. In the wooden world of the *Anson*, Robert received his initial lessons in seamanship and the proper deportment of a gentleman in the King's service. He also learned, first hand, about the realities of war. Britain was then battling revolutionary France and its allies, and the *Anson* saw its fair share of action. During the autumn of 1798 the ship was involved in the capture of two French frigates. In 1800 Captain Durham and his men took a French privateer, two Spanish gunboats and a half dozen merchantmen, cut out from under the guns of an enemy fortress. The next year the *La Furie*, another French privateer, was added to the list of prizes.

If he survived the rigors of war and the sea, a midshipman

As a newly appointed lieutenant, Robert Barclay (1785-1837) fought on the *Swiftsure* at the battle of Trafalgar.

could hope for his eventual promotion to the rank of commissioned officer. Robert Barclay was lucky enough to make that step upward when he was nineteen years old. In December 1804, while serving in the Mediterranean at Malta, he passed the mandatory lieutenancy examination and two months later was called on board HMS *Victory*, where he appeared before Vice Admiral Lord Sir Horatio Nelson. Nelson signed Barclay's commission as lieutenant and sent him to HMS *Swiftsure*, a 74-gun, ship-of-the-line.

As fifth lieutenant on the *Swiftsure*, Barclay took part, on October 21, 1805, in the battle of Trafalgar. Considered to be one of the greatest sea battles in history, Trafalgar brought Nelson a glorious death at the moment of his thundering victory over the combined fleets of France and Spain. Like the thousands of British tars who were present, young Barclay could ever after claim to have fought with Nelson on that fateful day. Barclay's likely station, during the frantic hours of that event, was a battery of cannons on one of the smoke-filled lower decks of the *Swiftsure*. Cutting into the enemy line late in the conflict, the *Swiftsure* engaged the French cruiser *l'Achille* and suffered seventeen men killed and wounded. During the violent storm that followed in the wake of the battle of Trafalgar, some of the heavily damaged French and Spanish warships, captured as prizes, were lost. The *Swiftsure* was involved in one of those tragic episodes. It had taken the French *Redoubtable*, the ship from which Nelson's mortal wound had been fired, in tow when that ship began to founder. Members of the *Swiftsure*'s crew made repeated trips in open boats to bring the prize crew and hundreds of French officers and seamen off the sinking ship. As fifth lieutenant, Robert Barclay would have been involved in that perilous business and would have watched helplessly as the severity of the storm made further rescues impossible and the *Redoubtable*, with some of its crew still aboard, was swallowed in the night by the merciless sea.

Following Trafalgar, Robert Barclay remained aboard the *Swiftsure* until it returned to England during the fall of 1807 for a refit, at which time the officers and crew were paid off. He took the opportunity to travel to Scotland, his first visit home since leaving in 1798. There he found things radically changed. His mother had died and his father had remarried. Barclay's brothers were no longer at home, since they were both serving in the military in India.

In spite of all the other junior Royal Navy officers looking for employment, Lieutenant Barclay was soon able to gain assignment to the 38-gun frigate *Diana*, under repair at Portsmouth.[2] Captain Charles Grant began his commission aboard the *Diana* at the end of October and took the frigate to sea in January of 1808. With Barclay as second lieutenant, the *Diana* patrolled the Biscay coast, where there were plenty of opportunities for action. In the month of March 1808, for instance, the ship took or destroyed eighteen vessels. During that same year, in an unsuccessful action against a French convoy, Barclay was hit by a ball from a swivel gun and suffered the wound that caused the amputation of his left arm just below the shoulder. In those pre-anesthetic days, when little thought was given to the sterile conditions of a naval operating theatre, amputation often led to a slow and painful death. Lieutenant Barclay's constitution was robust enough, however, to allow him to withstand the trauma. He recuperated aboard ship and began receiving a pension in 1809 for his loss. A second incident that occurred during his time on the *Diana* almost claimed Barclay's life. A six-oared cutter that he was taking to Ramsgate upset in rough water, leaving the lieutenant and seamen clinging to the overturned boat. Luckily their lateness was noted, and a search boat managed to find them. The *Diana* left the home waters in 1809 to voyage to Rio de Janeiro for the purpose of carrying Vice Admiral Sir Sidney Smith home from his post there. In August the *Diana* reached Spithead, at which time it is likely that Barclay left the frigate.

In 1809 Robert Barclay made a brief visit to King's Kettle. This time he returned home with his left sleeve empty and pinned to the breast of his uniform coat. He also arrived with the news that he was being sent to the North American station at Halifax on promotion, which meant that it was only a matter of time before he would be promoted to commander and given a ship of his own.

Unfortunately a tedious delay faced Robert Barclay when he arrived at Halifax. There were no ships immediately available that were suitable for him to command and to increase his frustration, he did not have enough influence with his superiors to be considered for an early placement. As a result, he was assigned to be the first lieutenant aboard the frigate *Aeolus* and, later, the frigate *Iphigenia*, cruising in the waters of the North American station.

On his promotion to commander, Robert Barclay was entitled to command a ship of fewer than thirty guns and was referred to as captain. Placement in a larger ship automatically included the advancement to the rank of post captain, an officer whose name was posted on the captains' seniority list. If he survived long enough, a captain could expect to rise up the seniority list and eventually be ranked among the admirals.

Barclay's wait for a promotion to commander lasted for the better part of four years. It was during a stopover at Bermuda in March 1813 that he received orders from Admiral John Borlase Warren to travel to Kingston, Upper Canada.[3] Once there, he would temporarily take charge as the senior officer for the Royal Navy on the northern lakes, with the rank of acting commander. It does not take much imagination to picture Barclay's joy at receiving the news. He was twenty-seven years old and could, at last, look forward to the opportunity of showing his worth with an independent command.

Barclay sailed for Halifax in the company of newly appointed Acting Commanders Daniel Pring and Robert Finnis. The former was bound eventually for action on the waters of Lake Champlain. Like Barclay, Finnis's fate would be met one sunny September day on Lake Erie. Untainted by foresight, the trio probably looked forward to commanding ships of their own, even if those ships would be stuck on the backwaters of the Canadian wilderness.

Durham boats ascending the St. Lawrence River

Travelling with the new commanders were six lieutenants: John Garland, George Inglis, Robert Gibbes, Miller Worseley, Thomas Stokoe and John Scott. All had been midshipmen in Warren's fleet prior to their promotions. Two former quarter masters, just appointed to serve as gunners on the lakes, were Thomas Williams and Daniel Sack.

Instead of sailing from Halifax to Quebec and from there to the lakes, the officers and men followed the "overland" route. This involved going by sea from Halifax to Saint John, from where boats were taken up the Saint John River into the heart of what is today the province of New Brunswick. The water route went as far as Lake Tamasquata, two day's march from the St. Lawrence River. Two weeks or more were spent with sailing up the St. Lawrence, trekking along rutted roadways and battling the rapids of the Lachine. Accommodation, in most cases, meant little more than getting out of the wind and cold by bedding down in a barn or rustic inn.

The arrival of the Royal Navy contingent at Kingston was anticipated with much urgent optimism. Sir George Prevost expressed his sentiments to Earl Bathurst, the colonial secretary in England:

> I have had the satisfaction of receiving information of the approach by land of several officers of the navy who have been sent from the Halifax Station to serve in the vessels now building on the lakes.

> Not a moment shall be lost after their arrival at Quebec in forwarding them to their destination, as their judgement and experience are essential to the completion of our preparations for ensuring our ascendency on Lake Ontario.[4]

Prevost had announced the imminent arrival of Barclay and his companions with a general order issued from his headquarters at Quebec on April 22.[5] The memorandum

24

Naval dockyard at Point Frederick

declared the understanding that the Royal Navy would be taking charge of the warships on the lakes, their crews and establishments on shore. The officers of the Provincial Marine would be reduced to lesser ranks, although they would "be suitably provided for without diminution to their Salaries." Furthermore, the general order predicted "the Brave Soldiers of Upper Canada will greet with heartfelt joy, the arrival of a Gallant Band of British Seamen."

Commanders Barclay and Pring reached Kingston near the end of April, the others following a day or so later. Whatever the nature of the greeting the party encountered, the senior officer wasted no time in reading his commission aloud before an assembly of the naval force and taking charge at Point Frederick, the shipyard at Kingston. Barclay assumed command of the *Wolfe*, a corvette of twenty-three guns. It was brand new, having been launched on April 28. Pring was given the *Royal George*, a 22-gun corvette and when he arrived, Finnis took command of *The Earl of Moira*, an aging brig armed with sixteen cannons. Also at Point Frederick was the *Prince Regent*, a 12-gun schooner, later rerigged as a brig. Another brig, the *Lord Melville*, was still under construction on the stocks of the shipyard. Besides the naval ships, a variety of smaller schooners and sloops served as transports in support of the squadron. To an experienced officer like Robert Barclay, this diminutive collection of three-masted, square-rigged corvettes, two-masted brigs and fore- and aft-rigged schooners, must have seemed rather insignificant in comparison to the great ships-of-the-line that cruised the oceans. Still, Barclay was favourably impressed with them. He wrote to Noah Freer, Prevost's secretary, that "the Ships are I think as fine vessels of their kind as I have ever seen. The *Moira* is small, it is true, but she is by no means so despicable as was represented."[6]

Barclay also had complimentary words for the efforts of Captain Andrew Gray. The state of the dockyard was commendable in Barclay's estimation, owing to Gray's efforts. He was not as impressed with the officers of the Provincial Marine, some of whom "appear[ed] to feel the loss of their commands more sensibly than was expected."[7] He predicted they would quit the service.

There was much work to be done at Point Frederick. The latest war news underlined the importance of preparing for a desperate struggle. The Americans were beginning the spring campaign with an all-out effort to gain supremacy of Lake Ontario. On April 27 Isaac Chauncey's squadron had conveyed General Dearborn's army across Lake Ontario to York, where they had routed the British garrison, destroyed the fort and pillaged the town. Furthermore, their attack had led to the destruction of the *Sir Isaac Brock*, a frigate under construction on the lakeshore, and the capture of naval supplies and military munitions meant for shipment to the Detroit frontier.

At Kingston, with the Americans obviously masters of the lake, the situation seemed grave. Commander Barclay went to work immediately to prepare the former Provincial Marine ships for battle and to increase the pace at the shipyard. He recommended that the keel for a new vessel be laid immediately at Point Frederick to compensate for the loss of the *Sir Isaac Brock*. "The Shipwrights from York furnish us with men," he suggested, "and Capt. Gray has with the greatest promptitude provided a sufficient quantity of wood (provisionally) to carry the project into execution, should it be approved of."[8] He also called for the construction of half a dozen gunboats. To effect these additions and to fit out the existing ships properly, Barclay submitted a list of materials ranging from anchors and rosin to whipsaws and brass locks. Priority items were asterisked and included four large stoves known as cabouses, twenty barrels of pitch and twenty more of tar, thirty coils of various types of rope and seven hundred weight of white, yellow and black paint.[9]

In the correspondence sent by Robert Barclay while he was at Kingston, there is evidence of his concern for the men who crewed his ships. Royal Navy seamen were accustomed to being given butter and cheese or cocoa and sugar, so the commander asked that these items be provided. "Tobacco is another great essential to the comforts of a seaman, the want of it would be severely felt, and there is none here ... I know that a seaman would forego

The *Sir Isaac Brock* on the stocks at York. During the April 27,1813 raid on York, the *Sir Isaac Brock* was burned and the dismasted schooner *Duke of Gloucester* (shown in background) captured and renamed *York* by the Americans. The masts in the picture belong to the *Prince Regent*, which was not present for the American attack.

almost any comfort rather than his tobacco."[10] The Royal Navy also clothed its crews, at an expense deducted from their wages. Evidently, an inadequate supply was in store at Point Frederick, since Barclay completed a requisition for slops, including 200 pairs of shoes, 100 hats, 100 thick, great coats and 100 flannel drawers.

Of Robert Heriot Barclay's personality and private life little information can be found. His portraits show a man who was proud and alert. His actions during the summer of 1813 give an indication of his competence as an officer and his view of the world. From one literary source we get a glimpse of how the one-armed commander from Scotland appeared to his companions and the people he served:

> [Barclay's] frame made up in activity what it wanted in height, and there was that easy freedom in his movements which so easily distinguishes the carriage of the sailor. . . . His eyes, of a much darker hue, sparkled with a lively intelligence, and

although his complexion was also highly florid, it was softened down by a general vivacity of expression that pervaded his frank and smiling countenance. The features, regular and still youthful, were of a plain and pleasing character; while neither in look nor in bearing nor word could there be traced any of that haughty reserve usually ascribed to the 'lords of the sea.' There needed no other herald to proclaim him for one who had seen honorable service than the mutilated stump of what had once been an arm.[11]

Those early days of May at Kingston, Upper Canada, were filled with great activity. There was a never-ending list of things to be done as the Royal Navy officers prepared to meet the challenge of facing the Americans on the lake. It must have been an exciting time for Robert Barclay, being the senior officer on the front lines of the war. That responsibility, though weighty, was one that every naval officer worth his commission yearned for. Acting Commander Barclay took on the task with zeal, but his efforts were soon cut short, for destiny awaited him in another place and under even more trying circumstances.

3

FROM KINGSTON TO LAKE ERIE

COMMANDER ROBERT BARCLAY'S term as a senior officer on the Great Lakes lasted less than three weeks. On the fifteenth of May 1813 his authority was superseded by the arrival at Kingston of Commodore Sir James Lucas Yeo.

Like Barclay, James Yeo was a veteran seaman, although his career had been marked by a more illustrious climb through the ranks.[1] He was born in 1782 and went to sea at age ten. He made lieutenant before he was fifteen years old and commander at the age of twenty-two. The naval actions in which he was involved earned him patrons in high places and notoriety in the British press. In 1807 he gained promotion to post captain and three years later, was knighted for the part he had played in routing the French out of South America. Yeo's reputation was substantial enough to help him through a court martial inquiry into the loss of the frigate *Southampton* in 1812. While commanding that ship in the West Indies, he had captured a privateer, and then suffered the embarrassment of running both vessels onto an uncharted reef. He was acquitted of all charges at the court martial held upon his return to Britain and was then handed the most prestigious command of his career.

Sir George Prevost's pleas for help in fighting the war with the United States had led to a decision by the government of Tory Prime Minister Lord Liverpool to send a detachment from the Royal Navy to Canada. Captain Yeo was selected to become the commander in chief on the Great Lakes. He sailed from Portsmouth late in March of 1813 aboard the *Woolwich*. Accompanying him on the troopship *Woolwich* were three commanders, eight lieutenants, eighteen midshipmen, six surgeons,

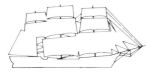

a dozen non-commissioned officers and four hundred seamen. They made the crossing in about five weeks, safely skirting the ices floes of the Gulf of St. Lawrence and arriving at Quebec on May 5. Three days later Yeo was in Montreal where he met Sir George Prevost. Together, they set out for Kingston by carriage and arrived there on the fifteenth.

One of Commodore Yeo's first acts at Kingston was to put Robert Barclay in charge of the gunboat division on the St. Lawrence River. He then considered which of his officers should be sent to assume command of the Provincial Marine squadron on Lake Erie. His initial choice for the job was Commander William Mulcaster. Mulcaster had served with Yeo in previous years and showed no hesitation in forthrightly declining the commodore's offer. Yeo then turned to Commander Barclay and ordered him to take charge of the Lake Erie establishment.

With little ado, Robert Barclay left Kingston during the fourth week of May—a departure which must have left him feeling

James Lucas Yeo (1782-1818) was promoted to post captain for the attack at Muros Bay, June 4, 1805, where he and only fifty men destroyed a small shore battery of cannons and attacked the fort (spiking its twelve cannons) in the town centre. He was knighted for the successful January 1809 seige of the fort at Cayenne, French Guiana.

very uncertain about his future. Although four warships and a number of lightly armed transports were anchored at Kingston, he was given only a one-masted "coasting" sloop (a craft that would have provided the absolute minimum in comfort) in which to travel up the lake to York. For defense the vessel was provided with a few muskets. The trip to York, which would have taken from three days to a week, must have been an anxious time for Barclay. The Americans had attacked York just a few weeks before and now controlled the lake, making the tiny sloop easy prey, should Chauncey's marauding squadron appear on the horizon.

During the voyage up the lake Robert Barclay had more than just Chauncey's ships to worry about. In spite of the more than four hundred Royal Navy seaman collected at Kingston, Commodore Yeo had sent him to Lake Erie with minimal support in the way of manpower. As Barclay later recalled:

The American assault of Fort George and the village of Newark, May 27, 1813

I was ordered to proceed to that Lake [Erie], with three Lieutenants, one Surgeon, and Purser, a Master's Mate, and 19 Men, 12 of these were Canadians who had been discharged from his [Yeo's] own Squadron on Lake Ontario the others were the most worthless Characters that came from England with him."[2]

Edward Buchan was the senior lieutenant in the group that included Lieutenants Thomas Stokoe and John Garland and the warrant officers, Surgeon George Young and Purser J. Hoffmenster. The master's mate, probably a recently promoted midshipman, did not complete the journey to Amherstburg, for by the time the sloop anchored at York the anonymous master's mate was deemed too ill to continue and was sent back to Kingston. He might have returned aboard the sloop, since Barclay decided that the vessel was not safe enough for making the trip to Fort George at Newark, presently the town of Niagara-on-the-Lake. The American squadron under Commodore Chauncey had been seen across the lake, and the sounds of frequent gunfire had been heard from the direction of Niagara. Barclay embarked his men aboard bateaux in company with infantrymen of the Eighth Regiment and on May 26 began rowing along the shore towards Burlington.[3]

After a day of heavy bombardment of Fort George, the Americans began their second invasion thrust upon the Centre Division of the British line by landing near Newark on May 27. While some of Chauncey's ships continued the bombardment of the fort, several others landed General Dearborn's troops. Within hours the British were in full retreat from the area.

The bateaux creeping along the lakeshore landed at Twenty Mile Creek at noon on the twenty-seventh. Commander Barclay and his men left the boats and struck out overland in

31

the direction of Fort Erie, where they intended to meet the ship *Queen Charlotte*. After an exhausting march, the sailors managed to get as far as Beaverdams by 10:00 p.m., only to find out that the *Queen Charlotte* had been ordered to flee from Fort Erie so that the Americans would not capture it. At Beaverdams Barclay met Major General John Vincent, the commander of the forces on the Centre Division, and learned the details of the successful American invasion. There remained no choice for the naval detachment from Kingston but to join Vincent in retreat towards Burlington. Rather than boarding a ship for the final leg of the journey to Amherstburg, it seemed that a gruelling overland march was now the only means left for completing their trip.

During that same week, while Commander Barclay and his men were rerouted around the Niagara Peninsula, another event was unfolding far behind them that would directly affect their own futures. Sir George Prevost and Commodore Yeo had received word of the American bombardment of Niagara. Since they did not have enough men to render any appreciable aid to Vincent's retreating army, they decided to strike at Sackets Harbour, the American naval base, while Commodore Chauncey was occupied with supporting the effort at Niagara. Embarking the troops aboard the ships of the squadron and a collection of bateaux, Yeo and Prevost sailed to Sackets, which was just over fifty kilometres from Kingston. They arrived on May 28, but the winds were light and irregular and the decision was made to postpone the landing until the next day. This delay proved costly, as it allowed the Americans to assemble volunteers and reinforcements to repel the expected attack. As a result, at dawn on May 29 the bateaux and ships' boats full of British soldiers and sailors met a fierce fire when they attempted to make their landing. The inability of the warships to lay down a supporting barrage made matters worse, and by 7:00 a.m. the order was made to withdraw. Two American ships had been set on fire (the flames were promptly extinguished) and some American troops captured. Prevost, who, as captain general, had been in command, was forced to admit that the expedition had "not been attended with the complete success which was expected of it."[4] More than 250 men were killed, wounded or missing. Among the dead, the sole officer slain was Captain Andrew Gray, the acting deputy quarter master general who had kept such a close eye on the Provincial Marine.

Midshipman David Wingfield, one of the young officers who had come to Canada with Yeo, commanded a boat involved in the attempt at Sackets. In a memoir of his war experiences, he commented that "the place would have been taken without the loss of a single man had things been conducted as they ought: this failure caused a coolness between the Governor and the Commodore and at length developed into an open rupture."[5] Wingfield, who survived the war and continued with the Royal Navy on the Great Lakes until 1816, also recognized the effect that the failure at Sackets Harbour had upon other events on the lakes. "Had we succeeded in this expedition," he wrote, "Sir James Yeo would have been enabled to send a reinforcement of Officers and Seamen, to each of the above mentioned places [Lake Erie and Lake Champlain]."

George Prevost's handling of the affair at Sackets Harbour demonstrated that his skills of diplomacy considerably outweighed his ability to manage a combined operation. The episode also gave Commodore Yeo a harsh introduction to the realities of the war along the lakes. While Barclay and his Royal Navy contingent tramped toward Burlington, the events at Sackets Harbour and the invasion of the Niagara Peninsula aggravated the weaknesses in the

British defense of the province and produced setbacks that contributed to the debilitating shortages that would be experienced on the Lake Erie station during the summer months.

The retreat to Burlington brought with it added frustrations for Robert Barclay and his men, some of whom lost their baggage owing to disorderly conditions on the march and to, what the Scottish commander considered, "the many disaffected people that the country abounds with."[6] Barclay's group followed the road to Forty Mile Creek where they embarked in bateaux and rowed on to Burlington Bay. At that point, Barclay left the men in the chargeof Lieutenant Edward Buchan and struck off, probably on horseback and with an attendant or two, on the long road to Amherstburg. He left Buchan with orders to conduct the others to Long Point and to wait there until a vessel could be sent to pick them up.

Commander Barclay had barely begun his journey when he met a man who told him that two schooners and a transport were anchored at Long Point. Barclay immediately sent a note to Buchan to bring the men on as fast as possible and headed for Long Point with all speed. He arrived there about May 30 and was met by Buchan and the others on June 1.

The narrow spike of land known as Long Point was a favourite mooring place for the lakers, since the anchorage was a deep and secure holding ground and the marshes and sandy hills of the peninsula offered a natural barrier during stormy weather. Sheltered in the protection of Long Point was a string of settlements, including Dover, Port Ryerse and Turkey Point. Long Point was customarily used as a depot for goods intended for delivery to Amherstburg and beyond and the place from which troops destined for Amherstburg took passage. When Barclay arrived, he found the armed schooners *Lady Prevost* and *Chippawa* and the transport *Mary* swinging at their anchors. He took command of the *Lady Prevost*, considering it to be, at first appraisal, "a fine strong vessel", but little else impressed him.[7] After he had mustered and inspected the crews (the *Lady Prevost* was manned by thirty-three sailors and soldiers, the *Chippawa* by twenty), Barclay wrote to Commodore Yeo with an assessment of what he had seen and what he had been told about the rest of his new command. In very clear terms, he made the first of what would become a long series of requests for help:

> Thus you may observe that the state of the Squadron on Lake Erie is by no means so well manned and equipped as you were led to believe from report and candidly (with the exception of about 10) the men which I brought with me are but little calculated to make them better. Those men on board the *Lady Prevost* and *Chippawa* I have mustered and examined. Some even cannot speak English, all are Canadians with very few exceptions. . . . I hope you will see the necessity of sending me a reinforcement of *good Seamen* that by mixing them with these I have I may be able to perform any service with honor to ourselves and advantage to the Country.[8]

On June 2 Barclay, with his entire contingent from Kingston, sailed from Long Point aboard the *Lady Prevost.* The *Chippawa,* commanded by a Provincial Marine lieutenant named Frederic Rolette, was sent to escort the *Mary* back to Amherstburg, while Barclay steered the *Prevost* toward the southern shore of the lake for a look into the American shipyard at Presque Isle. Unable to do so because the wind blew unfavourably, Barclay reshaped his course for Amherstburg.

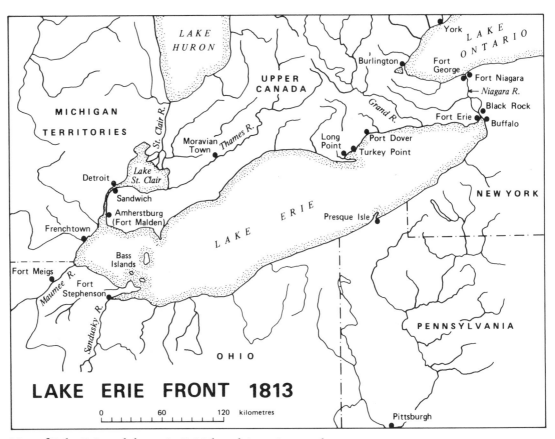

LAKE ERIE FRONT 1813

0   60   120   kilometres

Map of Lake Erie and the main British and American settlements

The *Lady Prevost*, carrying the senior officer for the Lake Erie squadron, came into view of the village of Amhertsburg on June 6, 1813. From the schooner Commander Robert Barclay saw the signs of the successful settlement that stretched along the eastern shore of the Detroit River where it emptied into Lake Erie. Dense stands of trees and a few windmills stood out on the flat landscape. Farm buildings were scattered across fields newly planted with corn and grain and among orchards of fruit trees that had just shed their blossoms. The *Lady Prevost* was steered northward against the current of the Detroit and up the deep channel between the narrow island of Bois Blanc and the mainland. Slowly the schooner glided towards the houses and the fort that composed Amherstburg.

For almost a century and a half Europeans had been following this same course.[9] Father Hennepin and the explorer LaSalle had come this way aboard the *Griffin* in 1679. In those days the land had been inhabited by native groups including the Pottawatomies, the Ottawas, the Wyandots and the Chippewas. Protecting their area of influence against the encroaching English, the French had sent Antoine Laumet Cadillac to establish a fort on the river in 1701. He chose a location on the western shore near Lake St. Clair. Using a native term meaning "the narrows", he called the fort Detroit. A settlement was established nearby and so was a Jesuit mission. That mission was later moved to Bois Blanc Island and then, in 1748, to a point across the river from Fort Detroit, where present-day Windsor is situated. In 1749 the first group of French settlers moved over to parcels of land near the Jesuit mission.

By the time the American states rose in rebellion against the English monarch, the area around Detroit had become more cosmopolitan. Scottish, Irish and English people added to the mainly French population. They had come to farm the land, to buy and sell, or to sail the lakes aboard the handful of ships involved in the merchant trade. When 1783 brought victory and independence for the United States of America, families that were still loyal to the Crown and wanted nothing of republican democracy flocked to Detroit from places as far away as New York and Virginia. A little more than a decade later they were forced to decide again about where they preferred to live.

Jay's Treaty, signed in 1794, separated British and American territory with a line drawn down the Detroit River. During the two-year period of adjustment that followed, Loyalists crossed over to resettle themselves on the opposite bank. Some chose to put down stakes at the village (later named Sandwich), opposite Detroit. Others selected plots further south, near the mouth of the river. British engineers had lately determined that the best channel for navigation ran between Bois Blanc Island and the mainland and that the narrow passage easily fell within the firing range of their cannons. Accordingly, they erected a fortification on a hillock overlooking the channel and laid out a townsite nearby. The fort and town were named for Lord Jeffrey Amherst who had been commander in chief of the British forces at the time of the conquest of French Canada in 1760. Later, the fort became known as Malden, after the township in which it was located. The first plan for Amherstburg featured three streets, cut parallel to the river, and two cross streets. It was laid out on land that had been for a decade or more the farm of a British veteran named Colonel Bird who had purchased the land directly from the local Indians, a pact which the authorities never officially recognized.

A road connected Amherstburg with Sandwich, situated twenty-five kilometres up-river. The road passed through the area known as Anderdon, which was controlled by the Wyandot Indians. At the commencement of the war, the local Indian population increased dramatically, as refugees from conflicts with American frontiersmen fled across the Detroit River to receive the support of the British. A large number of Shawnee warriors and their families were encamped on Bois Blanc Island.

When the *Lady Prevost* brought Robert Barclay to Amherstburg, the place had grown into a village of more than one hundred buildings, most of them constructed of logs and dressed lumber, a few of them of stone. They housed merchants and tradesmen and families with names like McKee, Duff, Clarke and Meloche.

The town was also dominated by two distinct sets of public buildings. One was Fort Malden, the name which the Americans used when also referring to the village. In the years leading up to the war, the fort had fallen into disrepair, a condition that was remedied promptly after President Madison's declaration. During the summer of 1813, Fort Malden featured barracks enclosed by earthen embankments and surrounded by a deep moat. On bastions protected by fraises were mounted as many as twenty cannons. The fort was the command post of Major General Henry Procter, who divided his time between there and the settlement of Sandwich. Centred also at Amherstburg was the Upper Lakes establishment of the Provincial Marine. Set up in 1796, it consisted of storehouses where items for outfitting the warships were kept and the work sheds where the naval artificers laboured.

Upon arriving at Amherstburg, Commander Barclay read the orders he had received

The village of Amherstburg, looking south-southeast, toward Lake Erie

from Commodore Yeo to the assembled officers and men on hand and promptly took command of the largest ship on the station, HMS *Queen Charlotte*. Lieutenant Edward Buchan was assigned to the *Lady Prevost*, while Thomas Stokoe, and probably John Garland, joined the *Charlotte*, since it was Barclay's intention "to make the Queen Charlotte as effective as possible in point of Officers that they may make up for the want of men in the event of being engaged in our looking into Presque Isle."[10]

Barclay's next task was to meet with Major General Henry Procter, whose position as commander of the Right Division made him Barclay's superior officer. Procter had begun his military career at the age of eighteen in 1781.[11] By 1812 his promotion had brought him to the rank of colonel in the 41st Regiment serving with Major General Brock. After the fall of Detroit, Brock appointed Procter to command the force at Fort Malden which, by the time of Barclay's arrival, was proving to be more than a little worrisome. As a consolation for the burden of command, Procter enjoyed the privilege of having his wife and children in residence with him. Undoubtedly, Commander Barclay and his fellow officers

36

were invited to dine with the Procters shortly after their arrival. It does not take much effort to imagine the men sitting around the dining table discussing the complexities of their situation late into the night.

The view of Amherstburg, looking north-northwest

Isaac Brock's defeat of General Hull at Detroit had been a great boost for the British morale, but throughout the winter the threat of William Henry Harrison's army advancing to reinvade Upper Canada hung over everyone's head. News reached Amherstburg that Harrison intended to build up a mammoth supply depot on the Maumee River (also referred to as the Miami River), from which he could later launch a full-fledged offensive. On January 18, 1813, before he could get well established, one of his subordinates, Brigadier General James Winchester, made the tactical error of routing a small British force from the outpost at Frenchtown less than thirty kilometres across the Detroit River from Amherstburg.

Four days later Henry Procter arrived from Fort Malden to challenge the Americans. With him came five hundred regular troops and militiamen and several hundred Indians. A surprise attack would have been the best approach for the situation in the wintry woods. Instead, Procter followed the slow and orderly rules of military protocol by forming his troops into proper battle lines. The rifles of the Kentucky troops in Winchester's regiments opened fire, inflicting great casualties on the British, but the accuracy of the American sharpshooters was not enough. Before the day was out Winchester's army had been severely crippled; four hundred were taken prisoner, another four hundred were dead or wounded. Only a handful straggled back to Harrison's main body. Procter withdrew quickly with almost 140 casualties among his own men. For the victory at Frenchtown, Procter received a promotion from lieutenant colonel to brigadier general. His casualities caused him concern as he reported to Sir George Prevost:

Major General Henry Procter (1763-1822)

I enclose a List of the Killed and Wounded. I lament there having been so many of Both, but of the latter a large Proportion will return to Duty, and most of them before too long. Before this Reduction of my Force I had too few, for the Defense of this Frontier. May I not hope that you will send me a Company of the 41st Regiment.[12]

Although set back by the Frenchtown disaster, General Harrison proceeded to fortify his position on the Maumee River by building Fort Meigs. By April his placement was well established. Meanwhile, Henry Procter had decided that an attack upon the fort itself would further impede the American offensive. Late in April he organized a force of more than 450 regulars (lately reinforced by detachments of the 41st Regiment), 400 militiamen and about 1200 Indians. The corps of infantry were transported to the Maumee aboard a convoy composed of Provincial Marine vessels and two gunboats, while the militiamen had to be satisfied with travelling in bateaux. Procter's force arrived within sight of Fort Meigs on April 28. For the next two weeks the opposing armies skirmished with and bombarded one another. On May 9 it became necessary for Procter to break off the engagement. His Indians were losing interest in the fight and his militiamen were clamoring to get home to their spring planting. Although nothing decisive had happened, Procter had been able to delay any American plans for a quick invasion of Upper Canada.

A VIEW of WINCHESTER in NORTH AMERICA *DEDICATED* to M^r. PRESIDENT MAD I SON!!
Extract from the Morn^g Chronicle Ap^l 23, 1813) It appears from One of the Halifax Papers, it was the famous Wyandot Chief ROUNDHEAD who took Genl Winchester Prisoner. The Indian according to his notion of the Laws of Nations, & Courtesy due to Prisoners of War, Stripped the American Commander of his Fine Coat, Waistcoat, &c. Shirt, & then Bedaubed his Skin with Paint. In this ludicrous state having dressed himself in his Regimentals, he presented him to Col. Proctor, who with difficulty Succeeded in getting the Discomfited Gen. his Coat, Sword & ba...

There is no doubt that Henry Procter was relieved to be joined by Commander Barclay and his men, despite the small number in his group. It meant that Procter would be able to place more trust in the naval arm of his defense of the Right Division of the British line. Not only was a huge army collecting near the Maumee River under General Harrison, but rumours about the ambitious shipbuilding program being conducted at Presque Isle under the leadership of Oliver Hazard Perry were becoming more ominous. It was just a matter of time before Perry united with Harrison to attack Amherstburg in the same way that Chauncey had helped Dearborn invade the Niagara Peninsula. Joined by a competent associate like Robert Barclay, Henry Procter could breathe a sigh of relief, even if it was only a shallow one.

The state of the American shipyard at Presque Isle was of foremost interest to Commander Barclay, but reliable information about the extent of the American building project was difficult to come by. "To put all conjectures past doubt," Barclay wrote to Yeo on June 7, "I intend going over there immediately to make such remarks and observations as may facilitate an Attack that may be made on that place."[13] A raid on Presque Isle would require reinforcements at Amherstburg, Barclay informed Yeo, and for the second time in a week he petitioned the commodore for more men.

During the evening of June 15 the *Queen Charlotte, Lady Prevost* and *Chippawa* arrived off Presque Isle. On their way down the lake, the British had been looking for enemy vessels said to be sailing upbound with reinforcements for General Harrison, but none had been sighted. They would have been coming from Presque Isle, where, since late in 1812, the

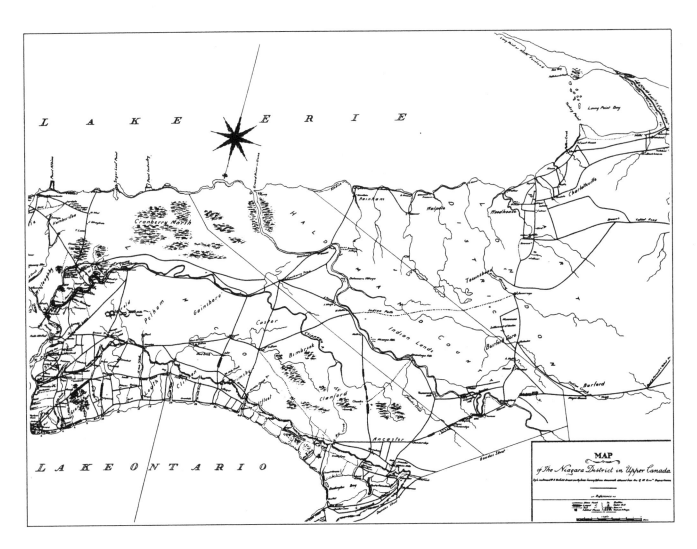

The Niagara District in Upper Canada

Americans had been building warships at the well-protected anchorage below the town of Erie. On the peninsula surrounding the harbour, hills and trees interrupted the view of the American building projects and a sandbar further protected the inner bay, so reconnaissance by the British was not easy. Commander Barclay directed his ships to pass near the mouth of the bay. From a lookout point high up the mainmast of the *Queen Charlotte* could be seen "2 Corvettes [actually a pair of brigs] with their lower Masts in and one with the fore rigging over, four Gun Boats and 2 small Schooners"[14] As well, the mouth to the harbour appeared strongly fortified with blockhouses and defended by hundreds of men.

Next day the British ships moored across the lake at Long Point where Barclay was pleased to find Acting Commander Robert Finnis and his steward waiting to be embarked. No other Royal Navy men had been sent with them, although there was a company of the 41st Regiment (which turned out to consist of only twenty men) within a day's march of

Long Point. Barclay wrote again to Commodore Yeo to update him as to the situation at Presque Isle. He did not mince his words regarding the needs of his squadron. "I need not I hope recapitulate what I have already written you about the Seamen I now have," he declared, "nor point out to you again the absolute necessity of having a few men that can be depended on . . ."[15] Barclay was eager to attack Presque Isle and made his case for reinforcements as strongly as possible. Too strongly, in fact, for the copy of his June 16 letter to Yeo bares a notation in the margin that the acting commander was sharply reprimanded for the tone of his language. That rebuke was the only immediate response Barclay's request earned.

Unaware of the effects of his plea to Yeo, Barclay also wrote to Lieutenant Colonel John Harvey, whom he had met at Beaverdams, and to Major General John Vincent to outline his plan for a raid on Presque Isle and to ask for their assistance.[16] To Vincent, he also sent congratulations for the June 6 victory at Stoney Creek during which the American invasion of the Niagara Peninsula had been abruptly halted.

The squadron left Long Point on June 17, with Robert Finnis superseding Buchan in the *Lady Prevost.* Later in the day the British ships were seen at anchor near a stream thirty kilometres east of Erie. Under cover of darkness that night, nine men deserted from the *Queen Charlotte* and subsequently gave testimony to Commandant Perry regarding the state of their former squadron. Early the following day Barclay and Perry came within cannon shot of each other, but did not engage. Perry was in the process of sailing a brig, three schooners and a sloop up to Erie from the shipyard at Black Rock when he received word from a man on shore that the British were in the vicinity. Perry prepared for action and was soon spotted by Barclay, but a thick fog began to envelope that portion of the lake, and although the squadrons came close to each other, no contact was made.[17]

Barclay returned to Long Point where the small company of the 41st Regiment was waiting. He embarked those twenty men, filled his ships and a transport with supplies and flour for the garrison at Amherstburg and then sailed with all speed for that destination. Despite the lack of immediate support from Yeo and the military, Barclay was still intent on putting his plan for dealing with the American shipyard at Presque Isle into action. The lack of suitable reinforcements was only one factor that interfered with his intentions, however. Waiting at Amherstburg was a tangle of problems that would add to the frustrations of the senior officer on Lake Erie.

4
OLIVER HAZARD PERRY, U. S. N.

WHILE ROBERT BARCLAY was beginning to familiarize himself with his new command during June 1813, the Americans continued with a shipbuilding program that had been going on for more than six months. Several hard-driving individuals had kept the ambitious efforts charging towards completion. One of those people was the young commandant from Rhode Island who, through his desire to serve his country, had won the assignment to command the new Lake Erie squadron.

Oliver Hazard Perry was born at Newport, Rhode Island, on August 23, 1785, less than a month before his eventual rival, Robert Barclay.[1] His sea career began in April of 1799 when he was made a midshipman and ordered to go aboard the frigate *General Greene*. He was following in his father's footsteps, literally, since the frigate was commanded by Christopher Raymond Perry. The elder Perry had gone to sea during the American Revolution. He later retired from the service, but volunteered to rejoin when a dispute developed in 1798 between France and the United States. Promoted to post captain, Christopher Perry was given the *General Greene*, in which he patrolled the West Indies, taking part in several minor actions. When hostilities with France ended in 1801, the American government reduced the size of its navy. Captain Perry went back to retirement, while his son was one of the fortunate young officers who was kept on.

Oliver Perry next served in the frigate *John Adams*, sailing in Mediterranean waters, and was promoted to the rank of lieutenant in 1802. During the next four years he sailed on the frigate *Constellation*, the schooner *Nautilus* and "Old Iron-

Oliver Hazard Perry (1785-1819)

sides" herself, the *Constitution.* Most of that time was spent in the Mediterranean and, although some of the Americans were involved in fights along the Tripolitan coast, Lieutenant Perry himself saw little action. In 1806 he returned home to Newport, Rhode Island, and was assigned to help in the construction of gunboats.

Still a lieutenant in 1810, Perry was given command of the schooner *Revenge.* In an unfortunate incident, caused by the misjudgement of a pilot, the *Revenge* was wrecked in

Long Island Sound in 1811. An inquiry into the loss ordered that Perry was not to be disciplined for the mishap, partly due to the fact that no one had died. He spent the following year ashore with his family, before being promoted to master commandant and given a flotilla of gunboats at Newport on the eve of Madison's war declaration.

Perry used the next few months to advantage, making sure the Navy Department did not forget him. It was his habit to send Secretary of the Navy Paul Hamilton any intelligence that he was able to pick up from blockade runners about shipping on the Atlantic and to keep the secretary apprised of his own efforts at Newport. On November 10, 1812, for example, he wrote to Washington with a description of how he had arranged for hospital quarters for the infirm among his crews since the gunboats provided no room for such amenities. On the same day Perry also reported the successful use of a diving bell during a salvage operation that reclaimed a 32-pounder cannon from a sunken gunboat.[2]

Oliver Hazard Perry was eager to serve in the style of the naval officers who had won fame and glory on the high seas like Isaac Hull did when he captained the *Constitution* to its victory over the British *Guerriere* in August of 1812. Perry's patriotic zeal and competence made him a likely contender for such honours. He was well respected by many of his contemporaries, one of whom was Usher Parsons, the surgeon's assistant from Maine, who joined Perry after his posting to Lake Erie. Forty years after the battle, Parsons was moved to remember Perry with this memorial:

> [He was] passionate upon provocation, aside from which he was the most exemplary officer I ever knew. Possessed of high-toned moral feeling, he was above the low dissipation and sensuality that many officers of his day were prone to indulge in. His conversation was remarkably free from profanity and indelicacy, and in his *domestic* character he was a model for every domestic virtue and grace. . . . On the subjects of history and the drama he was well read, and had formed opinions that evinced patient thought. He wrote with remarkable facility and in good taste. . . . He was the most remarkable man I ever saw for success in inspiring his officers with a reverential awe in his presence, and with a dread of giving him offense. Generous to the full extent of his means, his elegant hospitality especially on ship-board in foreign ports, reflected great honour on our Navy.[3]

There was little chance for glory at Rhode Island. The British blockade of the eastern seaboard had kept the American navy and merchant shipping fairly well hemmed in, leaving Perry, and many of his contemporaries, frustrated by the lack of action to be found in commanding a squadron of gunboats. Wanting a more challenging assignment, Perry wrote to Secretary of the Navy Paul Hamilton on November 28, 1812 to tender his "services for the Lakes."[4] He also wrote with a similar offer to Captain Isaac Chauncey. In January 1813 Chauncey sent a favourable recommendation to William Jones (who had replaced Hamilton as secretary of the navy), and on February 5 Jones formally gave Perry the opportunity he sought for active duty. He was to journey to Lake Erie where he would take charge of the American naval forces there. The appointment was a giant step for the twenty-seven-year-old officer who previously had only commanded a schooner and a group of gunboats and whose battle experience was extremely limited.

Undaunted by his lack of experience, Master Commandant Perry (the American rank of master commandant was comparable to the British rank of commander) wasted no time in setting out for the lakes. His orders had called for him to select members of his gunboat crews for service on the lakes. Within a week of receiving Secretary Jones's notice, Perry despatched three groups of fifty seamen each under the command of Sailing Masters Thomas Almy, Samuel Champlin and William Taylor to Lake Ontario. Perry left his wife at their home in Newport and travelled by sleigh in the company of his thirteen-year-old brother James, who was to become a midshipman. They crossed New England, stopping at Lebanon, Connecticut, to visit their parents and arrived in Albany at the end of the month.

In Albany Perry met Captain Isaac Chauncey. With the commodore he followed the water and land route that wound northward across New York State to Lake Ontario. During their journey Chauncey brought Perry up-to-date on the events that had developed since he had first arrived at Sackets Harbour. He explained the efforts that had been made by Daniel Dobbins and Jesse Elliot to put together a squadron on Lake Erie. Chauncey had visited the lake himself late in December, accompanied by the master shipwright, Charles Eckford. Eckford, who was supervising the building at Sackets Harbour, made recommendations about the types of ships that should be built at Presque Isle, and Chauncey authorized those plans. He also ordered Noah Brown, like Eckford a New York shipwright of excellent repute, to superintend the building at Erie. As Oliver Perry travelled toward the war zone, his Lake Erie squadron was well on the way toward becoming a reality.

Chauncey and Perry arrived at Sackets Harbour on March 3, 1813. An attack by the British was expected at any time. Accordingly, Perry and the crews he had sent from Rhode Island were held at Sackets to aid in its defense. Within two weeks that threat waned and Perry departed, leaving most of his seamen and officers behind. He arrived at Buffalo on March 24 and at Erie on the twenty-seventh, taking up residence in the Erie Hotel before beginning to familiarize himself with his new command post.

The peninsula of Presque Isle offered a perfect anchorage for shipping. A spindly neck of land wrapped around the harbour almost enclosing it. The narrow opening to the bay was too shallow to allow the entry of any large warships, and thick woods on the peninsula shielded the anchorage from strong winds. The French had erected a small fort on the site in 1749 and the Americans built a block house there in 1794. The hamlet of Erie was founded the next year and, by the time of the war, boasted a population of four hundred.

At Erie Commandant Perry met with Daniel Dobbins and Noah Brown. Both men were busily employed in the building of the new ships. Dobbins had been on the job since the fall and by order of then Navy Secretary Hamilton, had laid down keels for four gunboats, intended to be 15.5 metres long and 5.1 metres wide.[5] The visit to Erie, made by Isaac Chauncey and Charles Eckford on December 31 changed those plans. Eckford recommended that the size of two of the gunboats should be increased. Shortly after the new year, Eckford also produced plans for a pair of brigs, which Chauncey sent on to Erie. The keels to those vessels were laid, and with the arrival of Noah Brown early in March, the work moved ahead steadily.

During his first days at Erie, Dobbins and Brown informed Oliver Perry about the progress of the building. Brown explained his need for more shipwrights and more materials. Dobbins, who had sailed the lake for twenty years, outlined the resources that the countryside could offer. Together, the three men mapped out the plan of action that would, in a

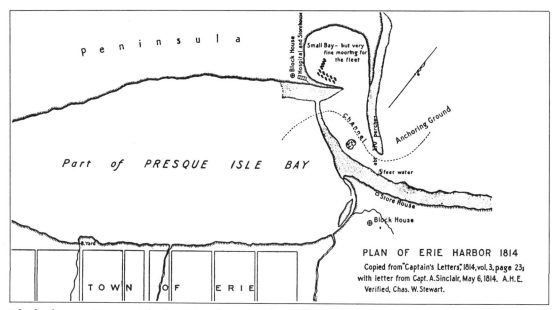

The harbour at Presque Isle Bay. Note how the channel weaves through the sandbar at the mouth of the bay.

remarkably short time, produce a powerful American naval squadron on the waters where none had existed before.[6] Perry quickly assumed overall authority for the project. Directing Noah Brown to push the building along as quickly as he could, he ordered Daniel Dobbins to depart for Black Rock and to begin ferrying naval ordnance, stockpiled there, back to Presque Isle.

Meanwhile, Perry intended to travel south to Pittsburgh where he hoped to find the materials needed to complete the squadron. He left Erie on March 31, after arranging with Major General David Mead, the local military commander, to have a militia force, numbering more than one thousand, encamped nearby as a defense against any British raiding party. Sailing Master Thomas Almy arrived at Erie on the thirtieth with thirty Rhode Island seamen, the first of several detachments of men from the Atlantic seaboard. In Perry's absence Almy was left in charge of the base.

Pittsburgh was perfectly suited to supply the needs of the new squadron. By 1812 it boasted a population of six thousand and a variety of industries so extensive that the smoke from busy furnaces clouded the air. Commandant Perry was able to contract for the fabrication of the rigging needed for the fleet at Pittsburgh's large ropewalk, which eventually supplied most of the cables and lines used in the squadron. Also on Perry's shopping list were cannonballs of various calibres, tons of iron spikes and bars and coal to fuel the smithies' fires in Erie. During his stay Perry met a group of labourers that had stalled there on their way to Lake Erie from the shipyard at Philadelphia. The carpenters, blacksmiths, sawyers and caulkers were hastened along, although the tools they needed had still not caught up to them.

While a portion of the building materials and ordnance that reached Presque Isle came through Buffalo from New York, Pittsburgh served as the point through which the bulk of

Daniel Dobbins (1776-1856) was a master mariner who initiated the shipbuilding at Presque Isle.

items for the Lake Erie fleet was funneled from the Atlantic coast. Overland, the distance from Pittsburgh to Erie was about two hundred kilometres. Travelling lightly, Perry took three days to make his journey, which was comparatively fast, considering the season of the year and the ravaged condition into which the roads had been cut by the trains of heavy wagons. A more circuitous, but smoother route was the course following the Allegheny River as it zigged and zagged northward to French Creek. The French Creek flowed past Meadville (where other steel mills were in operation) and onwards to Waterford. High water levels in 1813 made navigation possible for heavily laden barges right up to Waterford, from where an improved turnpike had been built to cross the final twenty-one kilometres to Erie. Teams of draft horses hauled the consignments down the rolling turnpike in mammoth Conestoga wagons. Despite the relative ease of the route, transportation of essential resources through the untamed forests of Pennsylvania was still excruciatingly slow. Noah Brown complained that he had almost finished building the ships before the materials he needed for them arrived.[7]

While Commandant Perry made his contacts in Pittsburgh, Daniel Dobbins was busy bringing materials from Black Rock. During April he made several round trips to that place, lugging ordnance at first by horse and wagon and then in open boats on the recently thawed lake. The trek was incredibly arduous, not to mention risky. At one point, as the lake swells rocked the decrepit Durham boat, which had been procured for transporting two 32-pounder cannon weighing a tonne and a half each, it became clear to Dobbins that he, his crew and cargo were in peril of foundering. Rather than give up, Dobbins "took a coil of rope they had on board, and securing one end forward, passed the rope round and round her fore and aft, heaving each turn taut with a gunner's handspike: and in that way, kept her together and afloat, all hands bailing."[8]

By the first week of May 1813, Erie was a madhouse of activity. Close to one hundred men were cutting and hauling timber, which went green and wet directly to the dockyard. Two hundred men worked on the six ships under construction. Each work day began at dawn and ended at dusk, if it didn't stretch on into the night. For that amount of effort a blacksmith could expect $2.00 in pay. A ship's carpenter earned as much as $1.25. The average wagoner got $2.50 for himself and his team of horses. Two large barn-like structures had been put up

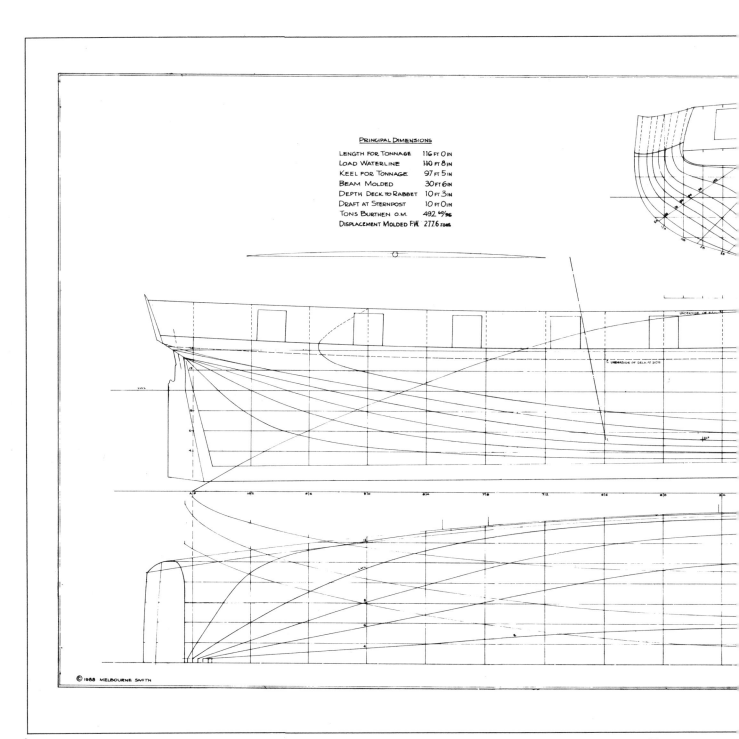

PRINCIPAL DIMENSIONS

LENGTH FOR TONNAGE	116 FT 0 IN
LOAD WATERLINE	110 FT 8 IN
KEEL FOR TONNAGE	97 FT 5 IN
BEAM MOLDED	30 FT 6 IN
DEPTH DECK TO RABBET	10 FT 3 IN
DRAFT AT STERNPOST	10 FT 0 IN
TONS BURTHEN O.M.	492 69/95
DISPLACEMENT MOLDED F.W.	277.6 TONS

© 1988 MELBOURNE SMITH

Original plans for the *Niagara* and *Lawrence*, drawn by Charles Eckford, were lost. These drawings were prepared by Melbourne Smith for the 1980s reconstruction of the *Niagara*.

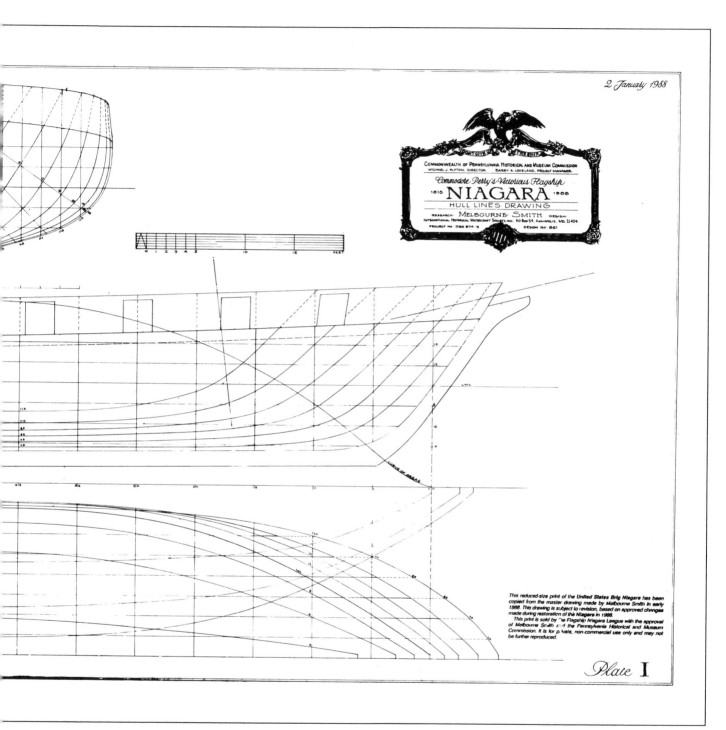

COMMONWEALTH OF PENNSYLVANIA HISTORICAL AND MUSEUM COMMISSION
MICHAEL J. RIPTON, DIRECTOR   BARRY A. LOVELAND, PROJECT MANAGER

Commodore Perry's Victorious Flagship

NIAGARA
1813   1988
HULL LINES DRAWING
RESEARCH· MELBOURNE SMITH ·DESIGN
INTERNATIONAL HISTORICAL WATERCRAFT SOCIETY, INC. P.O. Box 54, ANNAPOLIS, MD. 21404
PROJECT No. DBS 874-5   DESIGN No. 861

Plate I

to house most of the labourers. Others were billeted in private homes. Control was maintained on the cost of items sold in town, so the price of living was manageable. Food supplies were rarely cause for concern.

All four of the new gunboats were safely afloat on Presque Isle Bay by the third week of May. Their launch had been slowed by a delay in a shipment of oakum needed to caulk their seams. The twin brigs, which had been constructed at a site further west from the smaller craft where the water was deep enough to allow their launch, stood ready to go down the slip. During the final days of May and the beginning of June the brigs were launched, some difficulty being experienced when the stern of the second hull grounded heavily upon some debris on the harbour bottom. After considerable effort, both brigs were soon at anchor and being readied for sea. In the five months since the brief visit of Chauncey and Eckford, an incredible amount of work had been accomplished.

While the launching of the brigs was going on, Oliver Hazard Perry was absent once more from the Erie shipyard. Instead of seeking men and materials, however, the energetic young commandant had set out with Daniel Dobbins in an open boat heading for Buffalo and toward two escapades that brought him into proximity with Robert Barclay.

Word had arrived in Erie that a combined operation by Major General Henry Dearborn's infantry and Chauncey's fleet at Niagara was imminent, and Perry wanted to be part of the action. He and Dobbins left Erie on May 23, arrived in Buffalo the next day and hurried on to Fort Niagara. The journey involved nearly 150 kilometres on the lake and down the Niagara River to Fort Schlosser near Grand Island. From there the road was covered, through a rain storm, on foot and horseback.

Perry arrived at Niagara in time to participate in the May 27 attack on Fort George and the town of Newark. During much of the action he took up station in a ship's boat directing the firing of the naval batteries. At a critical point in the battle, he helped to steer the landing force safely to shore amid a lethal British fusilade. The day ended with the American capture of Fort George and the British in full retreat toward Burlington. Perry's actions had influenced the success of the attack, which in turn had critical repercussions upon the British war effort. Had the American plan not been so successful the British would have maintained control of the peninsula, and if that had happened, Robert Barclay would have made an uneventful trip to Newark and then continued across the peninsula in order to board a ship at Fort Erie for the trip to Amherstburg. Instead, the combined naval and military invasion caused Barclay and his small detachment of Royal Navy men to alter their course. On May 27 the two men were only kilometres apart from each other—the victory of one influencing the fortunes of the other.

A British withdrawal from the Niagara River shoreline followed the May 27 battle. On the American side of the river the collection of vessels at the Black Rock shipyard was no longer in danger of bombardment from British batteries, which had been abandoned. Commandant Perry arrived at Black Rock on May 28 and found that Daniel Dobbins had already begun to prepare the schooners for their trip to Presque Isle.

Over the next week the vessels at Black Rock were outfitted for sailing, armed with guns and loaded with supplies. Soldiers were borrowed from Fort Schlosser to lend the muscle power needed between June 6 and 13 when the formidable task of moving the five ships into the lake was undertaken. Since the current of the Niagara River was strong, the wind adverse

"BILIOUS REMITTENT FEVER"

This malady was to incapacitate Commandant Perry repeatedly during the summer. He was not the only unfortunate victim of an illness that at some points was affecting one in every five men in the squadron. Details of the "fever" are imprecise and only a guess can be made as to its cause. Perhaps there was a particularly virulent strain of influenza being passed among the closely confined masses of men. Similarly, some insect-carried disease might have been spread among the Americans. It is also a likelihood that poor sanitation control led to the pollution of the drinking supplies of the squadron. The freshwater lake and its rivers served as a bountiful source for cooking purposes and drinking. It offered, just as easily, a perfectly convenient sewer system, one shared by men and the plentiful wildlife that inhabited the shoreline. Fecal bacteria, the invisible enemy of which Perry, his surgeons and men had no notion, might have been the culprit that eroded the strength of their fighting force from within. The commandant pointed toward that reason in a September letter to Secretary Jones: "The crews of the different vessels have suffered much from a complaint occasioned, it is supposed, by the water. Many are still sick."

and the ships heavily loaded, there was no other course but to haul the vessels by ropes up the river to the lake. Known as *kedging*, the operation was an exercise in back-breaking exertion. Usher Parsons was present during this undertaking and recalled that "it was a Herculean labor to drag these vessels by land up the rapids at Black Rock into the Lake, and required nearly a week with two hundred men, who warped them with ropes over their shoulders."[9]

When the five schooners were finally ready to set sail for Presque Isle, Commandant Perry fell ill with a complaint described as "bilious remittent fever."[10] Despite his sickness, Perry was forced to rouse himself from his cot aboard the *Caledonia* during the trip to Erie when the British squadron was sighted. What evolved was the cat-and-mouse game played in the mists off the Lake Erie shore on June 18 that brought Barclay and Perry into close contact once again. An engagement at this point might have changed the shape of the summer's events and even the course of the whole war, but fate kept the opponents apart. Perry brought his flotilla safely to the Presque Isle anchorage on the morning of June 19 and wrote to William Jones, secretary of the navy, next day:

> I have great pleasure in stating to you, sir, that one of the sloops [a term used synonymously with *brig*] of war will be ready for service in a few days provided one bower anchor . . . and the shot arrive. . . . I shall bend sails day after tomorroe. Great delays have arose for want of iron of a proper size. . . . I shall be ready to execute your orders the moment a sufficiency of officers and men arrive, with one sloop of war and nine smaller vessels.[11]

Just ten months previously the single American warship on the lake had been surrendered at Detroit. Now, a fully potent fleet was nearing completion at Presque Isle and would soon be capable of showing its teeth to the enemy. From Black Rock had come the brig *Caledonia*, the schooners *Somers*, *Ohio*, and *Amelia*, and the one-masted sloop *Trippe*. On the Erie shore had been built the smaller gunboats *Tigress* and *Porcupine* and the larger-framed *Ariel* and *Scorpion*, altered by Eckford and Chauncey on their new year's visit.

51

Lastly came the main strength of the fleet, the brigs *Niagara* and *Lawrence*. The *Lawrence* was to be Perry's flagship, having been named after James Lawrence, captain of the frigate *Chesapeake* which had been taken on June 1 outside Boston harbour by HMS *Shannon*. Mortally wounded during the brief battle, Lawrence earned a share of immortality by saying to his men, "Don't Give Up the Ship." The *Lawrence* and *Niagara* (named for Dearborn's recent victory) were identical in dimension: 34 metres long, 9 metres abeam and drawing just less than 3 metres of water.[12] Their guns were mounted on a flush, upper deck. Below, because of their shallow draft, there was little space left for any amenities and no place to hide from cannonballs as they smashed their way through the hull. The commander's cabin near the stern was cramped and without windows. No ornamental woodwork, not even a figurehead, graced the brigs. Noah Brown justified these Spartan features by declaring, "we want no extras; plain work, plain work, is all we want. They are only required for one battle; if we win, that is all that will be wanted of them. If the enemy are victorious, the work is good enough to be captured."[13]

Decorative or not, the squadron would soon be ready to challenge the British for supremacy of Lake Erie. As the days of June stretched on, Oliver Perry waited impatiently for the final consignments of munitions and men to arrive, so that he could weigh anchor and take his ships out to battle.

5
PROBLEMS AT AMHERSTBURG

WHEN HE RECONNOITERED the American shipyard on his cruise to Presque Isle in mid-June, Robert Barclay witnessed the degree to which the Americans were intent on building a formidable squadron. Vessels were rigged and ready in the bay, the shore was crowded with men, and batteries covered the entrance. Three days later, as he cruised the south shore of the lake, he came close to intercepting a flotilla of five more American vessels sailing up from Black Rock. Although the British had maintained an armed presence on Lake Erie for years, it was clear that the naval force Barclay took command of in June was a poor match for the growing American threat. It consisted of only six vessels, for the most part, lightly gunned and inadequately manned.

Barclay's pennant flew at the masthead of the corvette HMS *Queen Charlotte*, at that time the largest and most powerful vessel on Lake Erie. Named in honour of the wife of King George III, it had been constructed at Amherstburg in 1809 by the master shipwright William Bell, a Scotsman who had arrived at Amherstburg in 1799 after learning his trade in the shipyards of Quebec. The three-masted, square-rigged ship was approximately 30 metres long on its flush, gun deck, 8 metres abeam and drew more than 3 metres of water. These dimensions combined to give the ship a burthen of about two hundred tonnes (a calculation that referred to the amount of cargo it could carry as opposed to its deadweight.)[1] During the summer of 1813 the *Queen Charlotte* was armed with a battery of eighteen 24-pounder carronades and due to its draught could not pass further up the lakes than the shallows of the St. Clair

Amherstburg in the summer of 1813, with Bois Blanc Island on the left. HMS *Queen Charlotte* sails up the Detroit River toward navy dockyard, where HMS *Detroit* sits on the stocks.

River.[2] Despite its good attributes, Robert Barclay considered the ship "very much smaller than I had an idea of. She is like the vessels on Lake *Ontario* more fitted as a packet than a man of war."[3]

From the viewpoint of fighting strength the *Lady Prevost* came next in line in Barclay's squadron. The *Lady Prevost* was rigged as a topmast schooner; its fore and aft sail arrangement being the most common among lakers of that period. Schooners required fewer men to manage them and could sail closer to the wind than square-rigged ships, making it possible

A model of the *General Hunter*, at Fort Malden Historic Park, reveals how the transport ship was armed for military use. The railings offered no protection from enemy cannon fire during the battle.

for them to navigate the many tight spots along the Great Lakes shores. The *Lady Prevost* was the newest addition to the Lake Erie Provincial Marine. It had been ordered in 1811 and launched during the summer of 1812 and measured about 22 metres long and 6.3 metres wide with a draught of less than 3 metres and a burthen of about 95 tonnes. Its armament consisted of ten short 12-pounder carronades and two long 6-pounders.

The *General Hunter* was the next biggest vessel in the Lake Erie squadron, although Barclay considered it "a miserably small thing."[4] It bore the sail configuration of a brig while under Barclay, although at one point prior to the war it had been rigged as a schooner. The *Hunter* was about 74 tonnes in burthen and carried a small battery of four long 6-pounder cannons and two 18-pounder carronades. The vessel, named for the former lieutenant governor of Upper Canada, Peter Hunter, had been launched in 1806 at Amherstburg, the third major project sent off the ways by William Bell. Before 1812 the *General Hunter* was probably used to carry merchandise for the lake trade. Only an open railing topped its sides, rather than stout bulwarks meant to withstand an enemy's broadsides. A long tiller was used to manhandle the small brig through the water. Late in 1811 the *Hunter* had been reported to be "fast falling into decay,"[5] and since it was the only warship at the Lake Erie establishment that could pass onto the upper lakes, a recommendation was made to replace it. Accordingly, work had gone ahead to build the *Lady Prevost*, which, with its shallow draught, was able to navigate safely the St. Clair River on the way to Lake Huron and beyond.

The rest of Barclay's squadron was composed of even smaller merchant vessels, converted for war service. The 35-tonne *Chippawa* was armed with two 8-inch Howitzers. The schooner had been built at Maumee in 1810 and captured by the British shortly after the war began. The *Little Belt*, formerly *Friend's Goodwill*, was a 60-tonne, single-master sloop with one long 12-pounder and one 24-pounder carronade. Lastly, the *Erie*, which was not used in the eventual battle with the Americans, had two guns, a long 12-pounder and a 12-pound carronade. The ordnance of these two sloops was mounted on pivots or traverses, which allowed the guns to be rotated for firing through most points of the compass. Both sloops had been seized by the British at Fort Michlimackinac in June of 1812. When Robert Barclay arrived at Amherstburg, the *General Hunter* was in the process of convoying the sloops south from Lake Huron. Perhaps it was Barclay who renamed *Friend's Goodwill* in honour of His Majesty's sloop-of-war *Little Belt*, which had been mauled by the large American frigate *President* during May of 1811. Two other small craft were at Amherstburg, the gunboats *Mary Eliza* and *Myers*, newly constructed during the spring. Propelled by oars and simply rigged sails, they were not deemed suitable for lake action.

Several other merchant ships had been requisitioned by the army for use during the war. These included the *Mary*, the *Miamis* and the *Nancy*, all of which were employed by Procter and Barclay for the transport of men and supplies. They had been built originally as schooners, with shallow drafts and wide holds for carrying loads of pelts, barrels of salt, bolts of canvas or casks of salt pork for the lake trade. The *Nancy* was a veteran among the fur traders, having been launched near Sandwich in 1789. After the eventual fall of Amherstburg, the *Nancy* became the target, in 1814, of a search on Lake Huron and Georgian Bay by the American squadron. As a last remnant of British shipping on the upper lakes, the *Nancy* sparked the incentive that saw a small contingent of Royal Navy men seek vengeance against the Americans.

One other vessel, the *Camden*, was moored near the shore at Amherstburg when Commander Barclay and his men arrived. The small snow-rigged *Camden* had been constructed at Amherstburg in 1804 by William Bell for the Provincial Marine. By 1812, the ship was in poor shape, having been declared "incapable of going to sea and even unfit to lodge the seamen during the winter."[6]

It must have seemed disturbingly obvious to Commander Barclay and his officers that their diminutive squadron was a poor match for the ships the Americans were collecting. One solution to that disparity was to conduct a building program that would rival the one at Presque Isle. When Barclay arrived in June there was work going on at the Amherstburg shipyards, but it consisted entirely of one new hull, that of a corvette, destined to become HMS *Detroit*. No other vessels were under construction, and even the work on the *Detroit* had not progressed as expediently as things had at Erie. Although Amherstburg *was* the site of the Lake Erie Naval Establishment, it lacked the resources available at the American port. In his June 7 letter to Sir James Yeo, Robert Barclay reported:

> The *Detroit* cannot be ready to launch in a Month at the least, the builder states that he is much in want of Iron to finish her—and there are neither Anchors nor Guns fit for her even when finished. There is a sufficient portion of Stores to equip her for immediate service, but will completely drain the Arsenal. There is no rope for the standing rigging made yet, but there is a sufficient quantity of hemp for that purpose and a very good rope maker.[7]

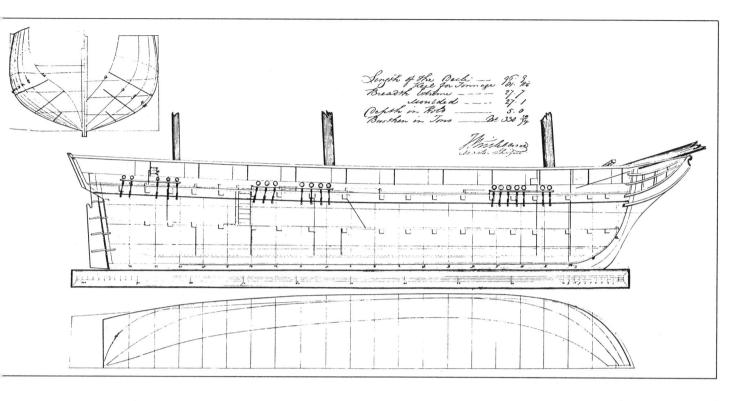

The
Admiralty
draught
for a ship
of the
Royal
George
class

The *Detroit* had originally been intended as a sister ship for the *Lady Prevost*. In November 1812, just months after the *Prevost* had been launched, plans were being made for laying down at Amherstburg another schooner with similar dimensions to bolster the strength of the Provincial Marine. By the end of the year, however, those plans had been altered by Prevost and his advisors. In order to keep pace with the shipbuilding efforts of the Americans, it was proposed that three ships be laid down immediately. The first was to be the 30-gun frigate *Sir Isaac Brock*, begun at York and burned during the American raid in April. The two other ships were identified as "Vessels of the Class of the *Royal George*, one at Kingston, and the other at Amherstburg."[8] The Kingston effort led to the launch on April 27 of the *Sir George Prevost* (quickly renamed *Wolfe*), captained by Barclay during his brief time there. The Amherstburg project yielded HMS *Detroit*, but as its sister ship slipped into the water at Kingston, the *Detroit* was a long way from being completed.

His Majesty's Ship *Detroit* was intended to carry sixteen 24-pound carronades and four long 12-pounders mounted in pairs at bridle ports in the bow and in the stern. The original draught for the *Detroit* has yet to be found, and William Bell's own working diagrams were lost or hidden away at Amherstburg during the final hectic days of September, so there are no precise descriptions of the size and shape of the corvette. Modern estimations, however, place the length of the *Detroit*'s main deck at just under 34 metres, the breadth at about 8.5 metres and the ship is thought to have drawn 3.7 metres of water and featured a burthen of three hundred tonnes.[9]

Waiting on the stocks, the hull of HMS *Detroit* nears completion

The *Detroit* had the potential to become the most powerful battleship on the upper lakes, a power that Robert Barclay could have used immediately upon his arrival at Amherstburg. Although the keel had been laid in January, work was still dragging on into June. One reason for the delay was a lack of materials necessary for the building. The naval yard at Amherstburg contained storehouses for the many items needed to keep the ships of the Provincial Marine afloat, but at the time of the building of the *Detroit* there was a shortage of such materiel. Just as Barclay had completed a "needs" list upon his arrival at Kingston, Henry Procter, early in January, had authorized an estimate of items that would go into the construction of the ship. On the list were amounts of white and black paint, linseed oil, various types of blocks, copper sheets and nails and iron in almost every size and shape.[10] Most of these items had to be imported from England. Being situated at the extreme end of the long and thin supply line, the shipyard at Amherstburg was left in a state of perpetual want. To make matters worse, that supply line could be pinched off if the Americans succeeded in sweeping the whole of the Niagara Peninsula and holding York. Oliver Perry, without the real worry of his supply route being threatened, was able to make arrangements at Pittsburgh for the production of ship fittings and munitions of all descriptions. Robert Barclay lacked this vital resource, since there were no industries in Canada comparable to

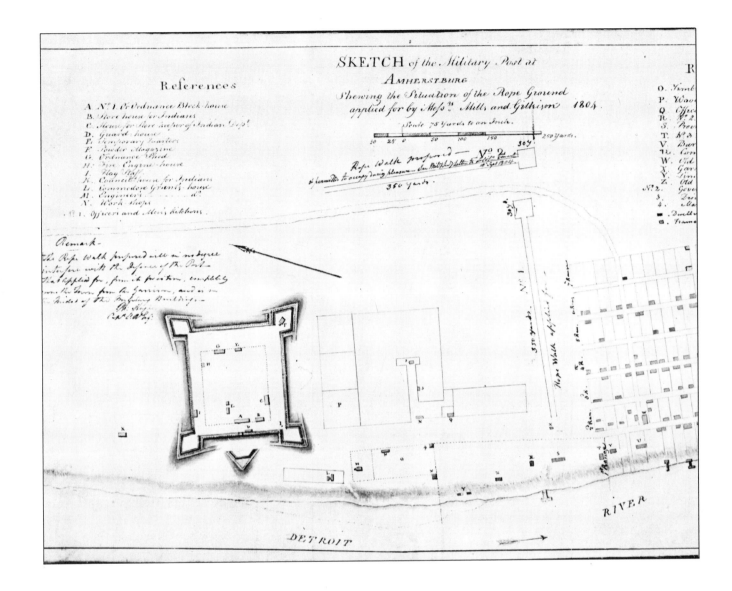

those found in the American centres. Iron, for instance, was not yet being fabricated in Upper Canada; the first attempt at smelting steel west of York did not take place until 1817, and even then proved a failure.[11]

Providentially some materials *were* available for William Bell's use. Suitable stands of oak stood on Indian property near Amherstburg and red cedar was cut at Pelee Island. As strange as it may seem, however, obtaining enough of the right kind of wood from the forests of Upper Canada could present some problems for an under-staffed shipwright. Not just any tree could be hacked down. Care was taken in selecting trees of suitable quality and which provided the shapes and sizes of lumber that would be needed.

Map of Fort Malden and Amherstburg in 1804 showing the location of two proposed ropewalks

A second resource available at Amherstburg was rope (as Barclay explained to Yeo). As early as 1804 a pair of men, named Mills and Gilkinson, had applied for permission to establish ropewalks near the village. Their proposal showed that each ropewalk featured a roofed, open-sided shed three hundred metres in length. At one end of the walk was a building where locally grown hemp was woven into cordage of varying diameters before being hauled down the walk.

Since the supply line was not dependable and the industrial resources of Upper Canada were virtually non-existent, William Bell probably had to rely heavily on his own creativity to fill the gaps in his storehouses. One of his solutions might have been to cannibalize the other vessels at Amherstburg. A suggestion to this effect had been made by Captain Andrew Gray in November when he commented that "the old iron from the *Cambden* will Supply the difficiency."[12] Although neither Procter nor Barclay described the use of the *Camden*, it seems reasonable to assume that the derelict and perhaps some of the transports were eventually robbed of parts needed to outfit the *Detroit*. As events turned out, the *Detroit* did finally sail into battle carrying borrowed equipment.

William Bell's construction problems extended beyond the matter of materials, since he also lacked the craftsmen required to do the job properly. Although the call had gone out early in the year to enlist men to help, insufficient numbers were available to move the work forward at a suitable pace. General Procter had complicated matters further by ordering Bell to focus his efforts during the month of March on the building of the two gunboats *Mary Eliza* and *Myers*. When Commander Barclay arrived, he found the shipyard hampered by labour unrest. Wages to the shipwrights, who had been brought from Lower Canada, were in arrears. Barclay acted quickly to have Deputy Assistant Commissary General Robert Gilmor arrange to pay the shipwrights' families through the Quebec headquarters.[13] The building continued, but at a slow pace, and by month's end Barclay protested to Major General Procter that "a party of 12 good shipwrights is also much wanted here—the builder represents that his present party are most ignorant of their profession—and the difficulties he labours under from that circumstance must be very great."[14] Barclay went on to explain that if he wanted to alter any aspect of one of his ships, or if a repair was needed, workman had to be taken from the *Detroit* to accomplish the task.

The shortage of manpower did not just affect William Bell's work. Robert Barclay also had great concerns for the numbers and calibre of the men who composed the crews of his ship. In his June 29 status report to Henry Procter, he stated his opinion bluntly:

> The absolute necessity of Seamen being immediately sent up is so obvious that I need hardly point out to you—The Ships are manned with a crew, part of whom cannot even speak English—none of them *seamen* and a very few even in numbers ... I have repeatedly pointed out to Commodore Sir James Yeo the manner in which the Squadron under my command is manned and I have no doubt of his sending as many seamen as he can spare—but I have little hopes of his sending a sufficient number, until some method is adopted to get another supply of good Seamen from England or Quebec.[15]

Looking after these men, considering the shortages becoming more noticeable at Amherstburg, was another priority for Barclay. He had already sent to Commodore Yeo for slops and fabric to clothe his crews.[16] Before he could set out from Amherstburg for the first cruise down to Presque Isle, it was necessary to ask Henry Procter to order Robert Gilmor to supply provisions for the crews according to the allowances normally issued in the Royal Navy. These included a weekly allotment for each man of two pints of peas, a half pint of oatmeal, six ounces of butter, six ounces of sugar, twelve ounces of cheese or cocoa and seven ounces of lime juice when no fresh beef was available.[17]

Besides seamen, Barclay also had to deal with the officers of the Provincial Marine. As he had done at Kingston, Commander Barclay appointed his Royal Navy colleagues to take the key positions of authority in his squadron, superseding the provincial officers. He was well justified in his actions. There was little doubt that a major confrontation was going to occur between his squadron and the enemy's. At such a time he would have to depend upon the competence of his brother officers, a competence that had been bred by experience at sea, the critical characteristic that the Provincial Marine officers and crews lacked. Few of them had cruised the Mediterranean or served on blockade duty in the stormy English Channel where great ships were handled in every sort of situation from reducing sail in a tempest to tacking in a line of battle. Naval tactics in the early 1800s generally followed strict routines, with the opposing fleets approaching each other in well-ordered columns. Once the fleets were engaged, such organization tended to fail as the fighting turned into a melee of crashing hulls, blasting broadsides and falling spars. When billows of smoke blocked any further orders from the admirals, daring officers were called upon to use their intuitions and expertise to make the right move at the right time. Undoubtedly, Barclay felt his brother officers were more capable of meeting such challenges than the members of the Provincial Marine.

Henry Procter shared Barclay's view. Early in January, as work was just beginning on the *Detroit*, he had written to Major General Roger Hale Sheaffe about the need for expert help at the Naval Establishment at Amherstburg. "In the rigging of the Ship," he wrote, "a Naval Officer should direct, and Sailors be employed. I do not believe there are either here properly qualified. I have taken it for granted that we are to receive Officers and Seamen from the only adequate source, the Royal Navy."[18]

The general order, issued by Sir George Prevost on April 22, had clearly stated that the officers of the Royal Navy would be taking over the marine establishments and that the officers of the Provincial Marine would be provided for without loss of salary. Commodore Yeo's lengthy instructions to Barclay had stipulated that he was to work in concert with Procter when organizing the squadron, make the best use of the available manpower, but above all, ensure that the systems followed in the Royal Navy be honoured.[19] Commander Barclay showed no hesitation in following those orders as he restructured the squadron. Between June and August some of the smaller vessels were left in the hands of Provincial Marine lieutenants, although the men of the Royal Navy, Finnis, Buchan, Stokoe and Garland, had the main authority in the squadron.

It appears that most of the Provincial Marine officers accepted the changes gracefully and continued to serve. Frederic Rolette, whom Barclay had met at Long Point, was a fairly experienced mariner. He had been present at the battles at the Nile and Trafalgar, before joining the Provincial Marine in 1807. Upon the declaration of war, he had almost single-handedly captured theAmerican brig *Adams* at the mouth of the Detroit River. During the winter he had fought with Procter at Frenchtown and been wounded. Robert Barclay eventually assigned Rolette to be first lieutenant under Edward Buchan on the *Lady Prevost.* Similarly, Provincial Lieutenant Robert Irvine had commanded the *Caledonia* when it was captured at Fort Erie in October of 1812. He, too, was wounded at the Frenchtown battle. By the end of the summer his assignment was on board the *Queen Charlotte* as second lieutenant. Rolette and Irvine, and others from the Amherstburg Establishment, appear to have accepted their placements and stayed with Barclay to fight at Put-in-Bay.[20]

One Provincial Marine officer who did not take reassignment kindly was George B. Hall. On recommendation of Isaac Brock, Hall had been made senior officer on Lake Erie in 1812, after Alexander Grant was retired from that position at the age of seventy-nine. Hall had commanded the *Queen Charlotte* during the barrage that preceded Brock's victory at Detroit. Over the winter he travelled to Quebec to enlist men for his squadron, but met with little success. In March of 1813 Andrew Gray suggested that Hall be given command of the *Detroit* when it was ready and,

Detail from Margaret Reynolds' watercolour of Amherstburg showing the *Queen Charlotte*

since he had a favourable opinion of the officer, urged that his being "retained at the head of this division of the marine will prove beneficial to the service."[21]

When George Hall's authority was superseded by the arrival of Robert Barclay, he applied to the new senior officer to be given command of a vessel. Barclay offered him a placement, probably in one of the small schooners or sloops, but Hall refused it on the pretense that it was not worthy of his rank of commander.[22] Hall obviously did not understand the significance of the arrival at Amherstburg of the men of the Royal Navy. He must have felt that the commendations he had received from Brock and Gray put him in a category separate from other Provincial Marine officers.

The dispute between Barclay and Hall festered through June and July. As preparations were made for the proposed raid on Presque Isle, Hall was the only Provincial Marine officer who refused to participate. Later, Barclay proposed to Yeo that Hall be made an attendant at the Amherstburg shipyard, a position that Hall accepted. By August when Robert Barclay was desperate to have every available man, he gave George Hall an ultimatum. "I have to demand a decided answer," he wrote on August 14, "whether you will serve or not—that I may strike a person off the Establishment [who] refuses to do the duty required of him."[23]

Commander Hall responded immediately with a politely worded declaration that he would serve readily in the "station and rank alloted me by His Excellency the Commander of the Forces [Sir George Prevost] and confirmed to me by Sir James Lucas Yeo."[24] (Yeo had already sent his approval for Hall's placement as shipyard attendant.) Hall's response cost him his job. The next day Barclay, in accordance with the discretionary powers in his orders, dismissed him from the Establishment and ordered Robert Gilmor to stop his "pay and other allowances."[25] Hall was not to be gotten rid of so simply. Without hesitation he wrote to the office of Sir George Prevost to explain his views of the situation and to ask for his attention to the case.[26]

The melodrama of the Barclay-Hall dispute was put to rest by a directive from Prevost's camp at St. Davids on the Niagara Peninsula. Through his secretary Noah Freer, Sir George indicated to Henry Procter that "the authority of Captain Barclay does not extend to annul any appointment which had received His Excellency's warrant nor should the pay and allowances of Captain Hall have been [stopped?] without your [Procter's] sanction."[27] Furthermore, it was ordered that Captain Hall be allowed to continue as attendant of the dockyard with proper remuneration. In other words, George Hall, unhappy with the change in circumstances, refused to take the position offered him by Robert Barclay and then went over Barclay's head with his complaint, ending up with a desk job and retroactive pay.

The post of senior officer on Lake Erie was fraught with a tangle of problems. The lack of sufficent ships and the crews to man them, and the additional burden of having to deal with obstinate personalities, while trying to stay on the right side of the sometimes confusing chain of commanders, posed quite a challenge for Robert Barclay. Such conditions could not have been entirely foreign to him, however. His nearly two decades of continuous service had placed him in all kinds of situations. The Royal Navy was huge; undermanned ships of war were commonplace and the need for new ships was continuous. Poor interpersonal relations among decision-makers frequently affected the events of war, so it is not surprising that, despite the difficulties he faced as naval commander at Amherstburg, Commander Barclay, after his first look in at Presque Isle, proposed a straightforward plan designed to put an end to the American threat.

6

THE FAILED BLOCKADE

FOR AN EXPERIENCED OFFICER like Robert Barclay, the best way to deal with the threat posed by the new squadron at Presque Isle was to attack that base and capture or destroy as much shipping and materiel as possible. With his warships and transports he could ferry Major General Procter's regiments to a landing near Erie and, while they stormed the town and its defenses, Barclay and his crews could use the small schooners or ships' boats to assault the American vessels. Meanwhile, the *Queen Charlotte, Hunter* and *Lady Prevost* could cover the parties with their broadsides. The raid would be typical of the "combined" expeditions that Barclay and the others had witnessed or taken part in many times.

Commander Barclay had suggested such a raid in his letter to Sir James Yeo on June 7. He had already discussed the scheme with Henry Procter who thought the plan was viable if he could obtain enough reinforcements to "enable him to leave this station [Fort Malden] with a competent means of defence against any attack that Harrison may make during the absence of the Ships and troops."[1] As an alternative to the use of the regular troops, Procter offered Barclay "a large body of Indians,"[2] but the commander considered that force, acting without Procter's disciplined regulars, ill-matched for the task at hand.

After his first look into Presque Isle, Barclay's opinion about the need for a swift and decisive attack was strengthened. He promptly expressed those views in letters to Major General Vincent and Lieutenant Colonel Harvey.[3] Again, to Yeo he wrote emphatically, "[f]rom the situation and appearance of the place [Presque Isle] (for I can get no positive information) a strong force will be requisite, at least 500 troops and with them I will get 1000 Indians from Gen'l Procter, with a proportion of

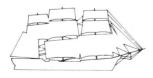

Seamen also from you—have no doubt of the success of any attack that may be made."[4]

About June 25 the *Queen Charlotte*, *Lady Prevost* and *Chippawa* returned to Amherstburg from Long Point. While he dealt with all the other concerns of his command (the *Detroit* was still far from finished), Barclay continued to promote the idea of the attack. John Vincent had supported his scheme and had written to Sir George Prevost to say so.[5] In Vincent's view destroying the American shipping, or even delaying its construction, would preserve British supremacy on the lake, which would in turn take some of the pressure off the urgent defense of the Niagara Peninsula. And, Barclay and Procter would have more time to prepare for whatever steps Perry and Harrison took to compensate for their loss.

On June 20 Governor General Prevost wrote to Henry Procter to tell him that he had personally ordered more than two hundred men of the 41st Regiment to be pushed on to Amherstburg.[6] He urged Procter to "encourage as much as possible the exertions of the navy; bring forward the united power of both services to crush the enemy's endeavours to obtain the ascendancy on Lake Erie, when a favorable opportunity presents itself." An important announcement also contained in the despatch was that Major General Francis Baron De Rottenburg had replaced Sir Roger Hale Sheaffe as commander in chief and administrator for the province of Upper Canada. With that promotion De Rottenburg became the immediate superior to John Vincent on the Niagara Peninsula and Henry Procter at Amherstburg. In consultation with Prevost, De Rottenburg began to select the priorities for the military forces in the province, a change in the hierarchy of command that directly influenced Robert Barclay's efforts to maintain supremacy of Lake Erie.

With reinforcements supposedly on the way and Sir George Prevost advising Procter and Barclay to work together, it looked as if the raid on Presque Isle was going to take place. Accordingly, the two commanders began preparing their forces. They embarked men, provisions and field ordnance on the ships. Meanwhile, they were waiting for the return of the *General Hunter* and the two former American sloops from Lake Huron so that they could be part of the task force when the reinforcements from the Centre Division finally arrived. As the days crept by Barclay, Finnis and the others met with Procter and his subordinates to discuss the particulars of their strategy for attack. July 4 came and went and still the men of the 41st did not appear. At some point during the next few days, however, bad news arrived; Major General De Rottenburg would not be sending the men promised by Prevost. Instead, De Rottenburg intended to use some of them in a foray against Black Rock, a post no longer of any real importance to the Americans.

Henry Procter barely controlled his wrath when he wrote to Prevost that he had been

informed that the Major General 'could not act in Conjunction with me and Captain Barclay on the Upper Lake at present; that he must first secure the Command of the lower Lake; after which there will be no Difficulty in recovering the Command of the Upper One.' With all due Deference, I beg Leave to dissent from the above. If the Means had been afforded me, which were no more than what Your Excellency has repeatedly directed should be sent to me, I could, in all probability, have effected the Destruction of the Enemy's Vessels at Presqu'isle, and have secured the Superiority of this Lake.[7]

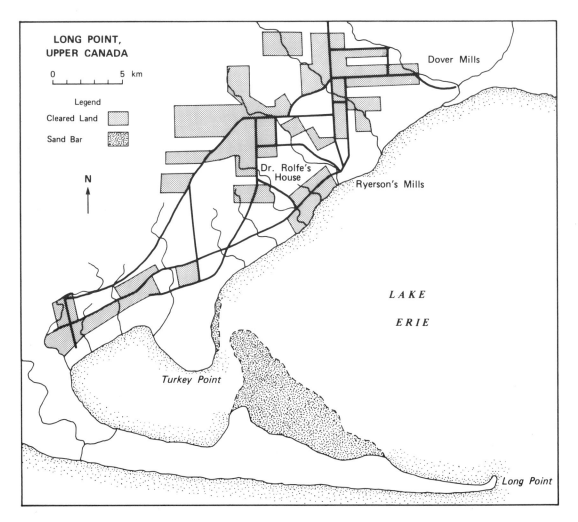

Long Point, Upper Canada

The plans for a joint attack upon the American post at Presque Isle were squashed. An attack that might have settled the battle for control of Lake Erie was stifled through a lack of support from Major General De Rottenburg. Perhaps, in the light of this frustrating predicament, a more daring military commander than Henry Procter would have proceeded without assistance and bravely taken the risk of joining Barclay in an assault on Erie, but Procter had a lot to lose by such action. His numbers were dwindling and even a victory would reduce his ranks further. As well, a sortie against Presque Isle would leave Amherstburg and Fort Malden unprotected with American General William Henry Harrison's thousands of men less than three days march away. What would happen if, on the successful return from Presque Isle, Procter discovered his own home base in enemy hands?

66

The situation at Amherstburg seemed unchangeably grim. It must have appeared to the military and naval officers that the Right Division was not highly valued by Prevost and the others. De Rottenburg had written to Procter on July 1 to tell him that, if the Niagara Peninsula fell, Procter could retreat with his whole force all the way up to Lake Superior.[8] There was little else for Procter to do but carry on, struggling with the supply problems and with the nagging of the Indians who were urging him to launch a second attack on Fort Meigs.

Rather than wait for more men, Robert Barclay resolutely decided to take his entire squadron out on the lake and he petitioned Henry Procter for a contingent of soldiers from the 41st Regiment to augment his ships' complements. Together with the officers and seamen he had brought with him, the members of the Provincial Marine, more than fifty men of the Royal Newfoundland Regiment and others from the 41st, he prepared to steer for Presque Isle "not only to prevent the Enemies Squadron from coming over the Bar but to be nearer Lake Ontario from whence I still fondly looked for re-enforcements."[9]

The British squadron, composed of *Queen Charlotte, Lady Prevost, General Hunter, Erie, Little Belt* and a transport, weighed anchor and slipped down the lake. On July 16 the ships were moored at Long Point. Waiting there were 120 men of the 41st and their commander Lieutenant Colonel Evans, ready to embark with the squadron. The situation on the Niagara Peninsula was improving and the Americans were more or less hemmed into the area around Fort George. Their most recent attempt to make a dent in the British defense had led to five hundred Americans being captured by a handful of British at the battle at Beaverdams on June 21. Barclay wrote to Sir George Prevost and to Commodore Yeo, reviewing the steps he had taken since arriving at the Right Division and repeating that he was still perilously short of men. If he was going to be able to make any stand against the Americans he had to have experienced naval reinforcements "even fifty would be of the greatest service for the present but it will require at least from 250, to 300 seamen, to render His Majesty's Squadron perfectly effective."[10]

From Long Point the British squadron cruised over to Presque Isle. Strengthened by the additional men of the 41st Regiment, Barclay had it in mind to attack any American vessels that may have crossed the bar.[11] He was disappointed to discover, still swinging at their anchors within the protective arm of the peninsula, the two new brigs *Lawrence* and *Niagara*, the brig *Caledonia*, seven schooners and a sloop. Barclay's ships taunted the Americans, prompting the militia to turn out in formation on the bluff above the harbour's entrance. From the shore the observers watched their enemies approach the bay, "their decks well covered with men . . . they passed and repassed immediately at the mouth of the harbour. . . . Commodore Perry and men enough to man one gunboat hoisted sail and played in front of them near the bar in hopes of getting a long shot, but the enemy steered a little out into the lake . . . and then shaped their course towards Long Point."[12] The British returned to Long Point on July 19.

Unfortunately, firing a few shots from one of his small gunboats was the best Oliver Hazard Perry could manage as a way of chasing off the offending British. Like Barclay, his independent command had not come without a slew of problems. He had been able to get his warships ready to sail, but he was frustrated by an inadequate number of men to crew them. He described his predicament to Navy Secretary Jones:

The British squadron at the mouth of the Detroit River ▶

The troops which were placed under my orders have returned to Buffalo by the express order of General Dearborn. I have not more than 120 officers and men fit for duty at this moment, there being upwards of fifty on the sick list. . . . As both sloops of war are now ready to go over the bar the moment a sufficiency of men arrive, I shall be able to meet them [Barclay's ships], and I trust, sir, the issue of a contest will be favourable to your wishes. I have boats at Buffalo to bring the men up.[13]

On July 21 the British hove into view once more. Barclay kept the station throughout the day, exchanging a few shots with Perry who had taken a couple of gunboats out to harangue the enemy. The next day the *Queen Charlotte* and the others were still there, but were seen to have "a number of boats with them."[14] It is unlikely that Barclay was thinking of making a boat attack upon the American fleet at this point, for he had written to Commodore Yeo two days before that he and Finnis had discussed the notion of an attack upon Presque Isle without substantial military assistance and decided "that to work an Action with so very inferior a force would be imprudent and impolitic in the highest degree."[15] No effort appears to have been made during this time to intercept any boat traffic coming up the lake from Buffalo, even though Perry received reinforcements by that route. Instead, Commander Barclay kept sailing back and forth near the harbour as a blockade to the American shipping that remained at anchor.

Commandant Perry continued to agonize over the predicament he perceived himself to be experiencing. "I cannot describe to you the mortification of my situation," he wrote to the secretary of the navy.[16] Not only was Barclay's presence posing a threat to his ships, Perry was beginning to get anxious requests to get his fleet over the bar and up the lake to support the efforts of General Harrison at Fort Meigs.[17] One of his great worries was being eased, however. On July 24 Sailing Master Stephen Champlin, three midshipmen and sixty-five seamen arrived, sent up from Lake Ontario by Commodore Chauncey. Six days later another band of sixty men and officers arrived. Perry complained that "very few of the men are seamen,"[18] but he decided anyway to take his squadron out as soon as the opportunity presented itself.

Unexpectedly, that opportunity had already arisen by the time the second large detachment of seamen reached Erie. From July 19 Commander Barclay's ships had kept a close blockade of Presque Isle, but abruptly on July 29 the British ships sailed out of sight towards Long Point. They did not reappear the next day nor the day after, and that was all the incentive Commandant Perry needed.

Early in the morning of Sunday, August 1, Perry took the fleet down towards the sandbar at the mouth of the harbour. The *Scorpion* and two or three of the other schooners were lightened and kedged over the obstacle, where they took up a defensive position should the British suddenly reappear. Next, the *Niagara* and some of the others were moored just inside the bar to form floating batteries. Thus protected and under the guns of a shore battery, the *Lawrence*, which had been emptied of its guns and stores, was eased down to the bar the next day. The wind was out of the east and the water level had fallen to just over a metre. Daniel Dobbins, who had buoyed out a course over the bar, piloted the flagship. The problem remained, however, to get the brig over the sandbar.

Before he had departed for Sackets Harbour, Noah Brown had supplied the solution for getting the brigs past the shallow entrance to the harbour. He had ordered the building of two huge scows, measuring 28 metres by 12.5 metres by 2 metres. These mammoth, floating boxes, or "camels" as they were called, were brought along either side of the *Lawrence* and with the opening of plugs, allowed to sink beside the brig. "Long heavy timbers were then shoved athwart the vessel through her ports, and strongly lashed to her deck frames and large ring-bolts in her side."[19] The timbers were secured to the camels, the plugs were reinserted and men began to push and pull on hand pumps, emptying the water out of the scows. As the camels rose in the water the *Lawrence* itself was lifted. Suspended between the wooden hulks, the brig was eased forward only to ground once more, causing the lengthy operation to be repeated. Early on the morning of Wednesday, August 4 the *Lawrence* finally floated in deep water beyond the sandbar, and "by two o'clock p.m. everything was replaced, guns mounted, a salute fired and she ready for action."[20]

Jesse Elliott (1782-1845) had fought on Lakes Ontario and Erie before the summer of 1813. His actions in the Lake Erie battle cast a shadow over the remainder of his life.

Work had already begun to lighten the *Niagara*. The remaining smaller vessels were moved out to the lake, leaving just the *Amelia* and *Ohio* behind to cover the inner harbour. With the *Niagara* halfway over the bar and the *Lawrence* still being rearmed, Barclay's squadron hove into view approaching Presque Isle. A fight seemed imminent, one in which the Americans, half ready, undermanned, and dropping with fatigue after days of continuous exertion, would have been badly mauled. Again, however, Providence was on Perry's side. Rather than attack, Commander Barclay directed his ships to turn away. Perry seized the initiative and ordered the *Ariel* and *Scorpion* to follow them. The British did not turn back to fight, choosing instead to disappear over the horizon headed for Long Point.

With all possible speed the *Niagara* and *Ohio* were brought safely over the sandbar and fitted out. Perry made final preparations and set sail on August 6, with most of his ships, crossing the lake for a quick look into Long Point and returning to Presque Isle the next day. At anchor off Erie, Perry received word that Master Commandant Jesse Elliott had been sent by Commodore Chauncey to Buffalo with one hundred men and officers. The *Ariel* was sent to collect them and arrived back on August 10.

VESSEL	TONNAGE	CREW	CANNONS	CARRONADES
Lawrence O. H. Perry	260	136	2 12–pdr.	18 32–pdr.
Niagara Jesse Elliott	260	155	2 12–pdr.	18 32–pdr.
Caledonia Daniel Turner	85	53	2 24–pdr.*	1 32–pdr.*
Ariel John Packet	60	36	4 12–pdr.*	
Somers Thomas Almy	65	30	1 24–pdr.*	1 32–pdr.*
Scorpion Stephen Champlin	60	35	1 32–pdr.*	1 24–pdr.*
Porcupine George Senat	50	25	1 32–pdr.*	
Tigress Augustus Conklin	50	27	1 32–pdr.*	
Trippe Thomas Holdup	50	35	1 24–pdr.*	
TOTALS		532	15	39

*armament mounted on pivots

The American squadron armed and manned as it sailed into battle on September 10, 1813.[21] The schooner *Ohio* was absent during the battle, having been sent to Erie for supplies. The schooner *Amelia* was declared unfit and did not sail from Erie with the fleet.

It was now time for Commandant Perry to organize his ships for their fight against the British. The quality of the men with whom he had to crew his squadron had caused Perry concern throughout the summer, and to a degree his worries were justified, given the responsibilities he shouldered. Most of his officers had next to no combat experience and some of his hands were volunteers from among the soldiers and landsmen. In Perry's favour was the fact that more than half of his ships' complements had come from the Atlantic seaboard and were familiar with the workings of warships. Among those seamen were a number of veterans sent from the *Constitution*, which was being refitted at Boston. With those men had come Lieutenant John Packet and Midshipman Dulaney Forrest both of whom had fought under William Bainbridge when he had taken HMS *Java*. Jesse Elliott, newly promoted to master commandant, was also well experienced in battle, having served through most of the year with Chauncey on Lake Ontario. The gang of men Elliott brought with him went straight into the *Niagara*, which gave that vessel, at least in Daniel Dobbins' view, the strongest crew in the fleet.[22] Dobbins, himself, was given command of the schooner *Ohio*, which later Perry used as a tender to the fleet, thus causing Dobbins to miss the clash with the British.

With his squadron suitably manned and powerfully armed, Perry distributed the orders of sailing among his officers, and on August 12 the anchors of the fleet were weighed. The ships stood out onto the lake, formed a double line and cruised away from Presque Isle to which they would not return until the control of the lake had been decided.

7
THE COMPLAINTS OF AUGUST

BY AUGUST 12 ROBERT BARCLAY'S ships were already swinging to their anchors in the Detroit River. Events appeared to be leading to a speedy confrontation with the Americans, and Barclay began to concentrate on "the necessity of at least making a Shew to prevent their [Perry and Harrison] taking advantage of their superiority and assailing us by land and lake together."[1] Very little appears to have been said, officially at least, about the fact that the British squadron had lifted its blockade long enough to allow Perry's fleet to enter the lake and then had failed to confront it. More than a year later, at his court martial proceedings, Commander Barclay dismissed that critical episode with the statement that he had covered Presque Isle as closely as possible until one morning he "saw the *whole of the* Enemies force over the Bar and in a most formidable state of preperation."[2]

What had caused the British to abandon their station off Erie just at a time when the Americans seemed ready to take to the lake? Apart from the clues in various observations and communications there does not appear to be a clear explanation for why Barclay took his entire squadron away from Presque Isle to anchor at Long Point on July 29. That same day Lieutenant O'Keefe of the 41st Regiment was sent to deliver a despatch to Major General De Rottenburg. The despatch conveyed several items of news. Word had reached the squadron that at Amherstburg the *Detroit* had finally been launched, although still left without guns. In addition, General Procter, bowing to the pressure of the Indian chiefs, had left that place on July 21 to undertake another attack on Fort Meigs.

A 1927 romanticized illustration of Barclay and the widow at Long Point. While Barclay dined, the story goes, the Americans slipped over the bar

Included in the message that O'Keefe carried was the explanation that weather conditions had caused the squadron to return to Long Point. Lake Erie is renowned for its ability to turn into a violently chopping sea that belies its small size and shallow depths. Although the

Americans made no mention of bad weather as they prepared to pass over the bar, a summer storm might had caused damage to Barclay's ships, making it necessary to seek the shelter of Long Point. There is some corroboration for this story. Upon arriving at Long Point, Barclay sent his carpenter to the local commissary to obtain spars of various lengths.[3] Perhaps the spars were needed to repair damage caused by rough conditions or a collision or the exchanges of gunfire with the Americans. Confirmation of inclement weather also comes from Amelia Harris, daughter of Captain Samuel Ryerse, who was an eyewitness to the struggle for control of Lake Erie. Years later in her memoir about pioneer life, she recalled seeing Robert Barclay and his second in command, Robert Finnis, at Port Ryerse when she had been a girl of fifteen. "When the weather was too rough for the Blockading vessels to remain outside of the Harbor," she recounted, "it was too rough for the American fleet to get over the Bar; consequently we felt very safe for the time."[4]

Two other stories add some further details to the episode. One comes again from Amelia Harris who recalled:

> There was a pretty widow of a field officer at Amherstburgh who was very anxious to go to Toronto. Capt. Barclay offered Her a passage in His ship and brought her to Ryerse and then escorted her to Dr. Rolph's. His fleet remained at anchor at Ryerse while He and some other of His officers spent a day at the Rolph's."[5]

Perhaps the pretty widow had been brought down the lake along with the news from Amherstburg, and Barclay, as an officer and a gentleman, agreed to convey her to Long Point. Regarding the day spent on shore, more information can be found in the biography of Daniel Dobbins. Dobbins' many years of sailing the lakes had earned him numerous acquaintances, from one of whom he heard that Barclay and his fellow officers had been given a public dinner at Port Ryerse. Apparently, the story went on, during that dinner the British commander had replied to a toast with a bold assertion that he would return to Presque Isle and find the American ships hopelessly stuck on the sandbar.[6]

It appears that a key reason for the extended layover at Long Point was to be on hand should the long requested reinforcement of seamen arrive from Lake Ontario. During the squadron's absence, sixty men of the Royal Newfoundland Regiment had arrived at Long Point and then proceeded by foot to Amherstburg. Barclay was waiting for seamen, however, and sent word to De Rottenburg on July 31 that "the moment the seamen arrived he would proceed to Brigadier General Procter, land the men of the 41st . . . and go immediately to Amherstburg to equip the *Detroit*."[7] A last conjecture about the lifting of the blockade is that Barclay had realized the futility of trying to blockade an apparently superior force. Clearly, he no longer had any intention of taking action against Perry at Presque Isle. He had written to Yeo on July 19 of his discussions with Robert Finnis about the feasibility of such an attack. They had decided that any confrontation would weaken their already fragile squadron and leave the Americans in complete control of the lake. Instead, Barclay had opted for returning to Amherstburg to work on the *Detroit* "and there remain until that Ship is fully equipped and Manned, that I may go out and meet the Enemy on more equal terms."[8] Later in that letter he petitioned the Commodore's empathy: "You will I hope acquit me of all blame in retiring before what I consider a very superior force indeed." Off Presque Isle on the twenty-first, Barclay prepared orders for George Hall, then superintending the shipyard, to keep

William Bell working steadily at the *Detroit* and alerted Hall that he was expecting to have to remove his force from the American port soon.[9]

After several days at Long Point, Barclay received word that about a dozen 24-pounder carronades were in transit from York to Burlington, but he could wait no longer for them or for more men. He weighed anchor for Presque Isle on August 4 where the Americans appeared to have surmounted the obstacle at the harbour's mouth and were ready for a fight. The sight of American ships beyond the bar caused Barclay in the *Queen Charlotte* to turn tail towards Long Point followed by the other vessels. Barclay wrote to Yeo to apprise him of the critical change in the situation on Lake Erie. His letter began with "The time is now come which I have so long feared that of being obliged to withdraw from this [place] without supplies."[10] He ordered the *Erie* to cruise near Long Point, hoping to receive news of reinforcements and to keep an eye on the Americans. Then he headed for Amherstburg.

August 4 was one of the most critical days in the summer's campaign. If Barclay had attacked Perry's ships at the harbour's mouth, only partially prepared for action as they were, he might have maintained supremacy on the lake for the rest of the sailing season. If he had maintained a close blockade, Perry might never have risked going over the bar. This last point was one that eyewitnesses like Amelia Harris did not overlook. "No one could have fought more bravely than Capt. Barclay," she wrote. "At the same time those who knew of His leaving the Blockade could not help feeling that all the disasters of the upper part of the Province lay at His door."[11]

Although the *Detroit* was afloat in the river and the work was proceeding to complete its rigging, little else had changed at Amherstburg by the time the squadron returned. In fact, things had actually gotten worse. Henry Procter had limped back to Fort Malden from an unsuccessful expedition against Fort Meigs and the American post at Sandusky. The ranks of his small army had been further thinned by the loss of fifty men killed or captured during the sporadic skirmishes with the troops of General Harrison. Disagreements among the British officers had made the operation more difficult, and the Indians, who had originally supported the attack, had not fought with any reliability.

The matter of keeping the stomachs of the Right Division filled continued to be a nagging logistical nightmare for Robert Gilmor. A letter written by him on August 6 to his opposite number on the Centre Division demonstrated the dire straits he was in.[12] Daily, Gilmor was responsible for providing rations for 15,000 mouths; 14,000 of which belonged to the throngs of native warriors who had come to the area in company with their families. There was wheat available for cutting, but "the two principal mills . . . are not now going— the dams are broke and . . . thus the wheat . . . will be of little immediate service to me for want of mills to grind it. The windmills at this season of the year do very little service." There was livestock to be found, but Gilmor had no money left to pay for it. Besides, some of the bills piling up on his desk had been caused by unbelievable acts of vandalism. He was waiting to give Procter "accounts to near two thousand pounds for working oxen, milch cows, sheep, hogs, etc. killed by Indians . . . Some of these cattle had been killed without any meat having been taken from them; in other instances the horns and tails seem to have been . . . cut off, the carcass is left to the dogs." Nor was there cash to pay the troops. Gilmor was beside himself with anxiety. He asked for a superior officer to be assigned who could take over. "I find more expected of me than all my abilities and zeal can perform," he lamented, "my accounts getting in arrears and the miserable prospect before me of . . . perhaps involving myself and my family in ruin for getting so involved." Like the commanding officers at Amherstburg, Robert Gilmor found his situation on the verge of being out of control.

Upon his return to Amherstburg, Major General Procter wrote again to Sir George Prevost, trying to explain the perilous future faced by the forces of the Right Division. The captain general, from his latest camp at St. Davids on the Niagara Peninsula, fired back a harsh response.[13] "Regarding the venture to Fort Meigs," he told Procter, "I cannot refrain from expressing my regret at you having allowed the clamour of the Indian Warriors to induce you to commit a part of your valuable force in an unequal and hopeless combat." In answer to Procter's request for reinforcements, he wrote, "You cannot be ignorant of the limited nature of the force at my disposal, for the defence of the extensive frontier." Then Prevost scolded Procter's slack reporting of events on the Right Division, which had prompted him to leave his regular headquarters to be closer to where he was obviously needed. Lastly, he swept aside Procter's concern about the Lake Erie squadron by declaring, "The experience obtained by Sir James Yeo's conduct towards a Fleet infinitely superior to the one under his command will satisfy Captain Barclay that he has only to dare and the Enemy is discomfited."

It is doubtful if Robert Barclay and his officers would have been very heartened by the idealistic opinions held by their commander in chief. Barclay, Finnis and the others were familiar with Yeo's circumstances on Lake Ontario. By late August they had undoubtedly heard that the Americans had made a second, half-hearted attack at York and that, in the days following that endeavour, Isaac Chauncey had lost four of his small schooners. Two of them, the *Hamilton* and *Scourge*, had foundered in a storm, while two others had been captured by Yeo. What Barclay may not have known for sure were the figures regarding the crews on the Lake Ontario squadron.[14] In mid-July Yeo had four ships similar in size to the *Detroit, Queen Charlotte, Lady Prevost* and *Hunter*, plus two more schooners roughly equal to the *Lady Prevost*. The crews for these six ships totalled more than six hundred men from the Royal Navy and the Provincial Marine. In addition, they were supported by two hundred soldiers serving as marines. Despite the apparent disproportionate strength of his squadron, Yeo had not yet seen fit to send any effective number of experienced seamen to Lake Erie.

The one bright spot in the otherwise murky situation at Amherstburg was that His Majesty's Ship *Detroit* had been launched without mishap. There could not have been a great deal of fanfare surrounding the event; Barclay had been at Presque Isle on blockade, while Procter had been preparing for the excursion to the Maumee River. Still, it was the end of a long and drawn-out building project. At least William Bell probably looked upon the launch and felt a proud moment, if not a sigh of relief. Maybe even George Hall saluted the product of more than half a year's work. As the *Detroit* lay in the river and the work crews completed the raising of its masts and rigging, Commander Barclay must have regarded the stoutly built corvette as the one trump card he could use against the Americans, if only Prevost or Yeo would send him the men and arms to do the job. Instead of more men, however, the next news Barclay received was that Perry's squadron had arrived at the Bass Islands, apparently ready for a fight.

In a double line, the American fleet had sailed towards the western reaches of Lake Erie, arriving at the Bass Islands on August 16. There it anchored in the shelter of Put-in-Bay after

The *Detroit* being outfitted at Amherstburg after its July launch. Borrowing from the other ships, HMS *Detroit* was ready to sail by the end of August. ▶

first chasing, but failing to capture, a British schooner, quite likely the *Erie*. The next day Perry moved his ships to Sandusky and sent word overland to General Harrison, who came on board the *Lawrence* on the nineteenth and spent the next two days with Perry and his officers. Their discussions determined that Harrison was not yet ready to commit his forces (numbering more than eight thousand strong) to a combined naval and military operation. He returned to his camp to make the needed preparations, leaving Perry with another thirty-five volunteers for his ships.

Those weeks of August 1813 should have been a time of great contentment for Oliver Hazard Perry. His tireless efforts had led to the creation of the most powerful armed squadron ever to sail the lake. The brigs and schooners, their hulls glistening with fresh paint, their sails bulging in the breeze, their guns ready like iron teeth to snap at the enemy must have been an awe-inspiring sight. And Perry, eager to serve his country and to be where the action was, should have been swelling with pride.

For Commandant Perry those August days were, in all likelihood, filled with some very contradictory feelings. On August 10, just two days before the squadron had departed from Presque Isle, Perry had written to Secretary of the Navy William Jones with a request to be relieved from his command. A dispute had arisen between himself and Commodore Isaac Chauncey over complaints Perry had made about the quality of men sent to him from Lake Ontario. To make matters worse, Chauncey had gotten wind of comments Perry had made to Navy Secretary Jones regarding the length of time it took for orders to arrive from Sackets Harbour.

The problem had begun in July when Chauncey received Perry's complaints and copies of despatches forwarded from Washington. Indignant, the commodore penned a very pointed rebuke to his second in command.[15] "I regret that you are not pleased with the men sent you," he wrote, ". . . for to my knowledge a part of them are not surpassed by any seamen we have in the fleet, and I have yet to learn that the colour of the skin, or cut and trimming of the coat can affect a man's qualifications." Regarding Perry's complaints to Washington, Chauncey asked, "Would it not have been as well to have made the complaint to me instead of the Secretary?"

Even though Commodore Chauncey assured Perry that "my confidence in your zeal and abilities is undiminished," the young commandant felt that he had been improperly chastised. "I cannot serve longer under an officer who has been so totally regardless of my feelings," he explained to Paul Jones.[16] His task at Erie had been a tough one as he tried to make the secretary understand: "I have been on this station upwards of five months, and during that time have submitted cheerfully and with pleasure to fatigue and anxiety hitherto to me unknown in the service." In the light of these unhappy circumstances, he asked to have his former command at Newport returned, or at the very least, to "be indulged with a short furlough, the situation of my family requiring my presence."

So, one month away from the event that would immortalize his name, Oliver Hazard Perry was pleading to be removed from his painful situation. Fortunately, for Perry's sake, the secretary would hear nothing of it. "It is the duty of an officer . . . to sacrifice all personal motives and feelings when in collision with the public good," Jones wrote, refusing the commandant's request. Then, in a curious turn of phrase, Jones assured Perry that it "is right that you should reap the harvest which you have sown."[17]

◄ **The British squadron moves down the Detroit River from Amherstburg to meet the Americans.**

Jones' reply, written on August 18, probably did not reach Perry's hands for more than a week. During most of that time, the American fleet remained at Sandusky. Another outbreak of illness had more than decimated its fighting strength. Scores of seamen, "the Commodore and half the officers were on the sick list with lake-fever."[18] Even Usher Parsons, the junior medical officer, was so sick that as he made rounds from vessel to vessel "he was unable to climb up the ship's sides, and he was hoisted in and out like a barrel of flour or a cask of water."[19]

By August 24 Perry's crews had managed to recover sufficiently to make it possible to weigh anchor and head for the Detroit River for a look at the British defenses. As the warships approached, all aboard them could plainly see that their arrival had been expected. The Queen Charlotte, Lady Prevost and the others had been moored across the river's mouth at a point where Bois Blanc Island was less than half a kilometre from the mainland. A strong battery had been erected at the tip of the narrow island. Beyond the ships could be seen the town of Amherstburg, Fort Malden and, moored in the river, the new corvette, HMS Detroit. Since the British seemed so well prepared, "Perry concluded it impracticable at that time to attack, and returned to Put-in-Bay",[20] where he and many of his men were once again laid low by sickness.

The British broadsides, primed and aimed, as they straddled the Detroit River with the settlement and fort behind them, may have looked menacing, but the truth was that the situation in Amherstburg was rapidly approaching a level of complete desperation.

With the supply line effectively cut by the presence of the Americans on the lake, Robert Gilmor was trying to make the final shipment of 670 barrels of flour last until the end of the month.[21] In the meantime he had sent men to Detroit, the Thames River and elsewhere to forage or buy whatever flour and corn and cattle they could find. If no relief was gained, soon all the military and its dependents were destined to be placed on half rations.

And still, no reinforcements arrived to help Procter and Barclay. Sending the squadron down to Long Point for supplies seemed out of the question with the American ships on the prowl. The British were not aware of Perry's hesitation to force a battle with his crews weakened by sickness or the time needed to get General Harrison's army ready for invasion. It was thought at Amherstburg that Perry might have already gone with Harrison's troops to storm Long Point. On August 29 Procter wrote again to Prevost, repeating his urgent appeals for more officers and seamen.[22] He tried to allay Prevost's fears "created by an anonymous correspondent"[23] that there was a lack of cooperation between Barclay and himself, and warned his commander in chief that he felt his Indian forces might abandon him if he did not soon receive the kinds of arms and implements that would help to buy their allegiance. In a word, the situation at Amherstburg was grave.

8
WAR COUNCILS

SEVERAL HOURS AFTER sunrise on September 1, the American squadron made its second visit to the mouth of the Detroit River. Perry brought his brigs and schooners in close to the British port to take a long and careful look at its defenses. As it had been ten days before, the British squadron was anchored in a line on the margin of the lake, but this time the tiny sloop *Erie* had been replaced by the "beautiful and very formidable ship" *Detroit*.[1] Upon the *Detroit* and the other vessels, the sight of the oncoming fleet had sparked a rattle of drums beating the men to quarters and clearing the ships for action. The frequent drills of the previous weeks had paid off and the crews were soon waiting in silence beside the guns that had been loaded and run out, ready to rebuff the oncoming enemy. In the stillness of mid-day the British watched, expecting the quiet to be torn asunder by the roar of broadsides and the cries of battles.

During their strategy sessions in the final days of August, the Americans had toyed with the idea of landing General Harrison's armies down the lakeshore twenty kilometres or so from Amherstburg. The various regiments could be loaded aboard the brigs and schooners and ferried in stages to the Bass Islands and then onto Middle Sister Island. From that place an assault on the British beachhead would have been effected by boats and bateaux, as Perry's warships covered the landing. Once Harrison's force was safely ashore Perry would take on Barclay's squadron. As ever in naval manoeuvres, the wind could spoil the best-laid plans, and it was the fear that an ill wind might bring Barclay driving in among the flotilla of landing craft that forestalled this particular invasion scheme. Before any similar invasion scheme could be put into action, the British squadron would have to be dealt with.[2] Perry's visit on

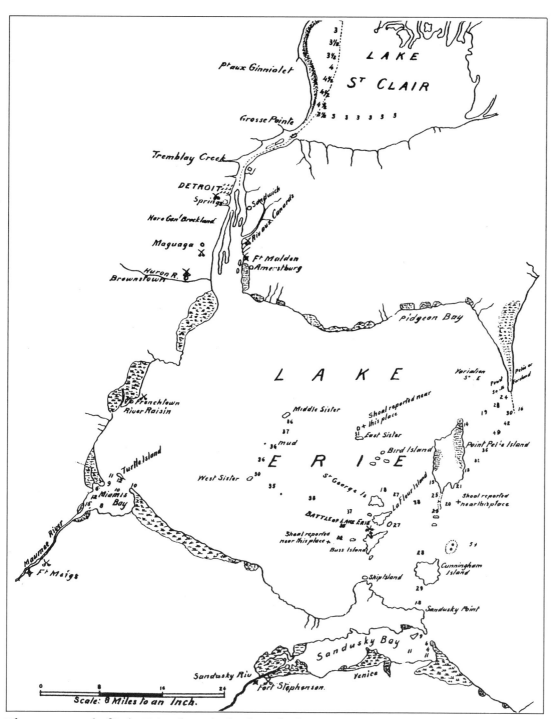

The western end of Lake Erie where the battle took place

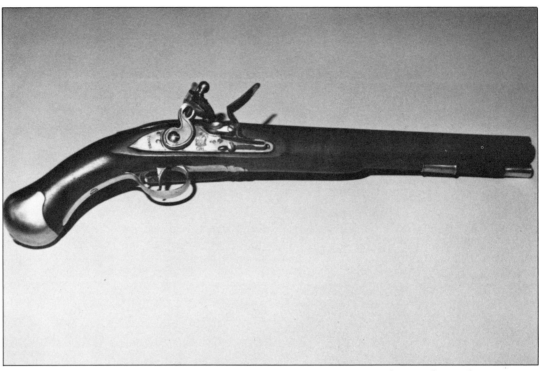

A replica of the type of sea pistol that the British sailors used to ignite the powder in their cannons.

September 1 had only been designed to reconnoitre the British position once more. After a good look, the Americans hauled off without firing a shot and returned to the Bass Island anchorage. Perry's ships were still weakened by the sickness incapacitating large numbers of their crews and the commandant had decided that it was not yet the time to fight.

Jesse Elliott put the blame for a lack of action squarely on Robert Barclay's shoulders. He showed no lack of contempt for his enemy when he wrote:

> We had the satisfaction to discover our opponents at anchor under their batteries at Malden with a force equal to ours. The new ship is all a taunto, and what keeps them in God only knows, for they have a third more guns. We have twice stood in, hove about and laid our topsails to the mast; waited two hours with the wind off the Malden shore. John Bull is not generally quick of comprehension, and I presume on this occasion will plead that as an excuse. Our desire was obvious.[3]

As the Americans disappeared over the horizon in the southeast, Commander Barclay must have thanked his good fortune. Just that morning he had written to Sir James Yeo to repeat the litany of problems he faced, the scarcity of able-bodied seamen, as usual, being foremost in his thoughts.[4] "I am sure, Sir James," he declared, "if you saw my Canadians, you would condemn every one (with perhaps two or three exception) as a poor devil not worth his Salt." He hoped that a portion of the crew from the troopship *Dover*, which he had just heard was being sent from Quebec to the lakes, would be forwarded to him. Not all of Barclay's note was full of gloom and doom, since he was able to express to Yeo his satisfaction with the quality of the *Detroit*. William Bell's craftmanship had created a sturdily built corvette that Barclay expected would give Perry's fleet a good chase.

With great exertions and a fair deal of creativity the flagship had been readied, at long last, to meet the Americans. As the original plan had stipulated, the corvette was "pierced" for a battery of sixteen 24-pound carronades and four long 12-pounders, but the weapons had not arrived. Some of the carronades had apparently arrived at Burlington, but with the enemy on the doorstep and the supply route cut off, it was futile to wait any longer for the guns to be sent to Amherstburg. As a result, Barclay and his officers met with Procter and agreed that the best solution to the problem was to reorganize the distribution of ordnance among the ships in the squadron and to strengthen the floating batteries with cannons from the earthen ramparts of Fort Malden.

VESSEL	TONNAGE	CREW	CANNONS		CARRONADES	
Detroit	300	150	2	24–pdr.	1	24–pdr.
Robert Barclay			1	18–pdr.*	1	18–pdr.
			6	12–pdr.		
			8	9–pdr.		
Queen Charlotte	200	126	2	12–pdr.	14	24–pdr.
Robert Finnis			1	12–pdr.*		
Lady Prevost	96	86	2	9–pdr.	10	12–pdr.
Edward Buchan			1	9–pdr.*		
General Hunter	75	45	2	6–pdr.	2	12–pdr.
George Bignell			4	4–pdr.		
			2	2–pdr.		
Little Belt	60	18	1	9–pdr.*		
commander unknown			2	6–pdr.		
Chippawa	35	15	1	9–pdr.*		
John Campbell						
TOTALS		440	35		28	

The British squadron armed and manned as it sailed into battle on September 10, 1813.[5]

*armament mounted on pivots

Through hour after hour the ponderous weapons were hauled from the fort to the ships and from vessel to vessel. The barrel of a single 12-pounder cannon weighed more than a tonne and a half, its carriage weighing just less than half that amount, making the chore of transporting the ordnance an awkward and dangerous one. Amid the choruses of grunting work gangs and the squealing of blocks, the guns were swayed aboard the ships followed by loads of shot and powder. At length the task was accomplished and produced some notable changes in the squadron that Barclay had inherited in June. The tiny sloop *Erie* was retired from active duty and moored near the town since there was "no Officer to command her."[6] The *Queen Charlotte* gave up four of its 24-pound carronades, which were replaced with three long 12-pound cannons, one mounted on a pivot. Alterations had been made aboard the other vessels, no doubt to maximize their fighting strength and to improve their sailing

In the chaos of the battle, firing the great guns with pistols was a disadvantage for Barclay and his men.

qualities. The most bizarre arrangement of weapons ended up on the *Detroit*; "a more curiously composite battery probably never was mounted."[7] Where a uniform set of carronades and cannons should have been, there were no less than six different calibres of guns, each type requiring its individually prepared powder cartridges and balls. In the chaos of battle the *Detroit*'s gunners would have the additional responsibility of matching the right projectile to each weapon. The hodgepodge of weapons left the gun deck cramped for space, room on the forecastle itself was probably taken up with the pivot and slide of the lone 18-pounder long gun.

Having the armament was one thing; teaching the largely inexperienced crews to use it to advantage was another. Commander Barclay issued a general order that the men were to be drilled at their guns twice a day for an hour or more at a time. Typical of the situation at Amherstburg, a shortage of powder required most of the drills to be acted out in pantomime only. Even then the carefully disciplined routine for loading, running out, firing and sponging out the smoking iron muzzles had to be amended. The cannons and carronades of that era were fired by means of a flintlock mechanism, which ignited the powder cartridge in much the same way as happened with a musket. Goose quills, or tubes as they were called, filled with powder, were commonly used to carry the flash of ignition to the cartridge. On Barclay's ships the quills, and even the flintlocks, were found to be so inadequate that gun captains were required to touch off their cannons by firing pistols at the vents. Some of the pistols themselves must have been defective since Barclay wrote to Procter asking that a sergeant of the Royal Newfoundland Regiment be sent from Sandwich to attend to their repair.[8] These inconveniences only helped to complicate matters.

Although the *Detroit* was armed, albeit in less than desired fashion, further alterations were needed before it was capable of sailing to meet the Americans. From the beginning, work on the ship had been delayed by a shortage of building materials, a situation that did not change. From the *Queen Charlotte* were taken "Stores of various Descriptions, even to Sails, Cables and Anchors, as well as a proportion of pistols to fire the Guns off with."[9] The British line that lay in wait as Oliver Perry's fleet approached on September 1 may have had a formidable appearance to some observers (with the exception of Jesse Elliott), but it was in reality rather a ragtag force, held together by make-do arrangements and a fair amount of determination.

The crews in the squadron matched the imperfect state of the ships. Halfway through August their commander was forced to appeal to Major General Procter for provisions that would allow the men to return to full rations and for them to be able to have as much firewood as the military troops did.[10] Barclay made repeated efforts to obtain money to pay his crews and officers and even requested that "a Bale of Red Cloth now in the Commissary's Stores . . . be supplied . . . for the use of the Crews."[11] It is quite likely that the British seamen went into battle dressed in newly made, crimson shirts and pants.

As the confrontation approached, both commanders were faced with the problem of how best to use the strengths of their respective squadrons when they finally came to battle. Barclay's own reconnaisance of the enemy was limited, as he had explained to Yeo on September 1:

> I have not sent any thing to reconnoitre them lately except a Canoe . . . fearing that from the frequent Calms, and their vessels being so well qualified to sweep they might take her [a sloop or schooner], and increase their force at our expence.[12]

Perry, on the other hand, had a more reliable notion of the weight of the British metal. Three men sympathetic with the American cause had escaped from Fort Malden and brought to the commandant news about the fire power of Barclay's ships. That information revealed that they lacked the balance of arms that Perry's ships had.[13]

Carronades and cannons were both used at the battle of Lake Erie. Cannons could fire their solid iron shot well over one thousand metres.

The batteries of the Americans were best suited to an action at close quarters. The sturdy bulwarks of the *Lawrence* and *Niagara* were meant to take the punishment they would sustain in such a melee, and the brigs were also perfectly equipped with their rows of 32-pounder carronades. The *Detroit* and *Queen Charlotte* could take their share of bruising too, but at close range the weight of their broadsides could barely match those of the brigs. To back them up the four other British ships were lightly armed. Their pop guns would offer little resistance against even a single broadside from the *Lawrence*, which could hurl three hundred pounds of steel, or more, if the guns were double-shotted. The crews of the schooner *Lady Prevost* and the others would be kept very busy anyway fending off the attack of Perry's schooners. Mainly armed with heavy, long guns, those vessels could keep up a steady bombardment from a distance, while the shots from the four smaller British ships fell short.

Barclay could take advantage of a weak link in the American armament, if a running fight developed that saw the American brigs and the British corvettes outsail their sluggish little consorts. If Barclay could capture the advantage of a sharp breeze and chase Perry, firing at him from beyond the 450-metre-effective range of the carronades, his long guns would be virtually unopposed. The *Lawrence* and *Niagara*, each with its pair of 12-pounders, could offer only a weak challenge to the *Detroit*. Unfortunately, the *Queen Charlotte*, with its main batteries of short-range carronades, did not equal the long distance strength of the flagship, and that fact underlined the imbalance in the British squadron. Besides, if the smaller vessels were left to fend for themselves in the streaming wakes of the *Detroit* and

Carronades required fewer men to handle them and were short-range weapons.

Charlotte what would become of them, outnumbered two to one by the brig *Caledonia* and the schooners? Although a running fight seemed to be the best alternative for the British, it was by no means a sure thing. Barclay and his officers might have considered the strategy of running their ships directly on board the enemy to wage a hand-to-hand battle. The reports of preparation for battle indicate, however, that efforts were concentrated on training for a broadside-to-broadside action. Clearly, Barclay planned to rely upon superior gunnery and, perhaps, a healthy dose of good luck.

BROADSIDE STRENGTH OF MAIN COMBATANTS IN THE BATTLE

	British Squadron			American Squadron	
VESSEL	**ORDNANCE**	**WEIGHT OF BROADSIDE**	**VESSEL**	**ORDNANCE**	**WEIGHT OF BROADSIDE**
Detroit	long guns	= 114 pds.	Lawrence	long guns	= 12 pds.
	carronades	= 24 pds. or		carronades	= 288 pds.
		18 pds.	Caledonia	long guns	= 48 pds.
Queen	long guns	= 24 pds.		carronades	= 32 pds.
Charlotte	carronades	= 168 pds.	Niagara	long guns	= 12 pds.
				carronades	= 288 pds.

LONG DISTANCE BROADSIDE = 138 pds.   = 72 pds.

SHORT DISTANCE BROADSIDE = 330 pds.
                                             or 324 pds.   = 680 pds.

BROADSIDE STRENGTH OF SUPPORT VESSELS

British Squadron			American Squadron		
VESSEL	**WEIGHT OF ORDNANCE**	**BROADSIDE**	**VESSEL**	**ORDNANCE**	**WEIGHT OF BROADSIDE**
General Hunter	long guns	= 16 pds.	Somers	long guns	= 24 pds.
	carronades	= 12 pds.		carronades	= 32 pds.
Lady Prevost			Porcupine	long gun	= 32 pds.
	long guns	= 18 pds.	Tigress	long gun	= 32 pds.
	carronades	= 60 pds.	Trippe	long gun	= 24 pds.
Little Belt	long guns	= 15 pds.	Ariel	long guns	= 48 pds.
Chippawa	long guns	= 9 pds.	Scorpion	long gun	= 32 pds.
				carronades	= 24 pds.

LONG DISTANCE BROADSIDE = 58 pds.   = 192 pds.

SHORT DISTANCE BROADSIDE = 130 pds.   = 248 pds.

The comparable strengths of the guns that could be brought to bear (ie. the broadsides) in the ship-to-ship actions that evolved during the battle. The *Detroit*, for instance, could hurl 138 or 132 pounds of iron in one broadside at close range (depending upon which side was engaged), whereas the *Lawrence* could counter with a 300-pound broadside. Alterations made during the battle offset these figures: Perry and Elliott both shipped their long guns to the starboard side at the opening of the battle; in both squadrons the guns were double shotted at times; and during the course of the action some guns were disabled.

Oliver Hazard Perry, resting at the Put-in-Bay anchorage, must have been aware of all the contingencies surrounding the upcoming battle. He reviewed with his commanders the way he expected the meeting with the British to develop. He intended to engage Barclay at close quarters and, since he expected the *Queen Charlotte* to lead the British line, he ordered Jesse Elliott to face that ship at the van of the American squadron. Perry would keep the *Lawrence* back in order to go up against the *Detroit*. Signals and other details were discussed and reviewed. The strength of the squadron was reduced by one as Perry despatched the schooner *Ohio*, skippered by Daniel Dobbins, to Presque Isle for supplies.

On the evening of September 9 Perry called his officers together aboard his flagship for a briefing during which he revealed for them a large battle flag he had ordered sewn. In tall white letters stitched upon a deep blue background were emblazoned the words "Don't Give Up the Ship," the dying words of James Lawrence, captain of the *Chesapeake*. He intended the flag to lead the fleet into action. With the intelligence regarding the strength of Barclay's squadron had come news "that the British force at Malden was very short of provisions, and that at a council of military and naval commanders, it was determined their squadron should sail, and give battle . . . or make the attempt to open communications with Long Point."[14] The battle for control of the waters of Lake Erie was imminent.

The story of a war council at Amherstburg was not exaggerated. The situation in that first week of September led the military and naval officers to conclude that something had to be done immediately. Either they could abandon the Right Division, burning everything in their flight or try to re-establish the supply line to Long Point. The people at Amherstburg, soldiers, sailors, citizens and Indians alike were rapidly reaching a point of starvation. Robert Gilmor's resources were about at an end with "only 300 bushels of Corn . . . in Store and 40 Barrels of Flour" and without any money, except what he could borrow.[15] With little choice, Gilmor sent a party by bateau to Long Point, despite the danger of capture by the Americans.

Henry Procter, too, was desperate. The Indians were causing him increasing concern, clamouring for the guns and ammunition, the blankets and other gifts they had been promised. To the Governor General's office he wrote "the Enemy . . . are not inattentive to any Circumstances respecting the Indians, that may be turned to their Advantage. I do not hesitate to say that if we do not receive a timely, and adequate Supply of Indian Goods and Ammunition, we shall be inevitably subjected, to Ills of the greatest Magnitude."[16]

Robert Barclay had written to Commodore Yeo again, this time with subdued thanks for the reinforcements that had finally arrived. It had come in the form of Lieutenant George Bignell, Lieutenant George Inglis, a master's mate, two gunners and thirty-six seamen, formerly of the troopship *Dover*, who had been transported down Lake Ontario by Yeo and landed at Burlington. The detachment of seamen was none too strong, some of them being only *boys*. Barclay distributed them among his ships, assigned Bignell to command the *Hunter* and Inglis as second lieutenant of the *Detroit* and, for the final time, summarized the situation for Commodore Yeo:

> That the Number [of new men] is tottally inadequate to render the Squadron under my command effective is well known to you, by representations I have already so frequently made. But it is the opinion of the Major Gen'l Commanding the forces here; that some thing must be attempted by me to enable us to get Supplies, by the Lake. . . .
>
> That such a thing is necessary, there cannot be a doubt and in consequence if I find that no farther re-enforcements are likely to arrive immediately, and I know something of the few that have arrived I shall sail and risk everything to gain so great a point as that of opening the communication by water.
>
> That the Risk is very great I feel very much . . . I am certain of being well supported by the Officers, which gives me almost all the confidence I have in the approaching battle.[17]

Commander Barclay waited three more days for help to arrive. When none came, he gave the order to weigh anchor at 3:00 on the afternoon of Thursday, September 9, 1813 and led his squadron, the forlorn hope of the British, away from Amhertsburg.

9
THE BATTLE

AT DAWN ON SEPTEMBER 10, 1813 the lookout perched on the heights of Gibraltar Point, one of the rocky outcroppings scattered among the Bass Islands, signalled to the American squadron lying at Put-in-Bay that ships were approaching from the northwest. Oliver Hazard Perry, realizing instantly that it was Barclay come out to fight, quickly passed the word for his vessels to weigh anchor.

The breeze was baffling and light as the American squadron struggled to leave its anchorage that morning. Besides being weak, it was also blowing from the southwest and that placed Perry at an immediate disadvantage. Usually the opening stage of any confrontation between warships under sail was taken up with careful manoeuvring by the opponents as each strove to make sure the wind was in his favour. Capturing the weather gauge (being between the wind and the enemy) allowed a commander to control how fast or slowly to press action, which left his antagonist with the choice of setting all sails and fleeing or fighting against the wind to get into a preferred position. That undesirable alternative, not unlike running up a hill to meet an enemy charging down, was the one that Perry chose rather than escaping downwind. Beneath a pristine summer sky the two squadrons plodded toward each other, their full sets of sails filling gently in the three-knot breeze. At 10 a.m. they were still more than five kilometres apart when that faint wind died away and abruptly returned, blowing this time from the southeast. Perry became the first recipient of good luck as the advantage of the wind gauge fell into his hands.

It was a moment of critical importance for the British. If they held their position and engaged, they were allowing Perry to set the scene and pacing for the battle. If the British tried to run, they might be able to escape, but to what effect? Robert Barclay, ever mindful of the need to relieve the supply shortages at Amherstburg, made his choice and ordered his commanders to lay to. Aboard each ship the men rushed to reduce and back the sails so that they brought their vessels to a virtual standstill in the water. Lying in close quarters at regular intervals, the *Chippawa*, *Detroit*, *General Hunter*, *Queen Charlotte*, *Lady Prevost* and *Little Belt* waited for the enemy to come downwind to them. From the American squadron, little could be detected of the difficult circumstances under which Barclay had left Amherstburg. Across the lightly rippled water, his ships appeared "all newly painted, their sails were new and their bright red ensigns were tending to the breeze, all looking splendidly in the bright September sun. Their appearance and movements showed that a seaman and master spirit held them in hand."[1]

Earlier Perry observed that the British had not formed the line of battle that he expected. As his squadron crept forward, he ordered the *Niagara*, which according to his strategy had taken the van, to heave to while the *Lawrence* caught up, whereupon he called over to Elliott that he would take the lead. *Scorpion* and *Ariel* were told to move ahead to support the flagship. With those changes the American squadron proceeded. At about 11:00 a.m., amid a chorus of cheers, Perry raised the flag bearing James Lawrence's heroic words to the masthead and then ordered the crews to be fed, since the normal hour for their meal would probably find them fighting for their lives.

Aboard HMS *Detroit*, Barclay, accompanied by Lieutenants John Garland and George Inglis and Provincial Lieutenant Francis Purvis, inspected his ship to ensure that unnecessary furniture and stores had been stowed out of the way and that cartridges and balls were on hand at each gun. Below deck the passageway to the magazine was guarded, the opening to the stuffy compartment itself shrouded with water-soaked fabric to prohibit any errant spark or flame reaching that highly inflammable storeroom. Just like in the Americans ships, the British crews were fed early and their meal topped off with the final draughts of spirits remaining in the ships' casks.[2] A stillness fell aboard the *Detroit* and its sister ships as the men consumed what many of them must have feared would be their last meals. Tidings of good luck and final bequests were given as the soldiers and seamen crouched between the guns on the deck, where sand had been spread intended to provide footholds later when the planks became streaked with blood. In the final tense moments as the Americans approached, led by one of their powerful brigs, Barclay looked over the ships of his command and perhaps gave a silent salute for success to his colleagues Finnis, Buchan, Bignell and the others.

Just before 11:45 a.m. a bugle sounded aboard the *Detroit*, followed by song and cheers along the British line. The ships in that squadron had reset their sails to get underway in a south-southwest direction. Perry's vessels, coming out of the southeast in a line that straggled across three kilometres of lightly rippling water, were altering course to run on a path parallel to their opponents. At 11:45, with the Americans about two kilometres distant, Captain Barclay gave the order to try a shot from *Detroit*'s long 24-pounder.

From the deck of the *Lawrence*, which Perry was steering to engage the British flagship, the smoke of the long gun could be seen drifting away on the light wind. A splash well ahead of the brig showed where the ball had fallen short. The American crews waited stoically for their turn to reply. A few minutes later a second puff of smoke appeared on the larboard side of the *Detroit*. There was a pause lasting several moments and then the ball smashed through

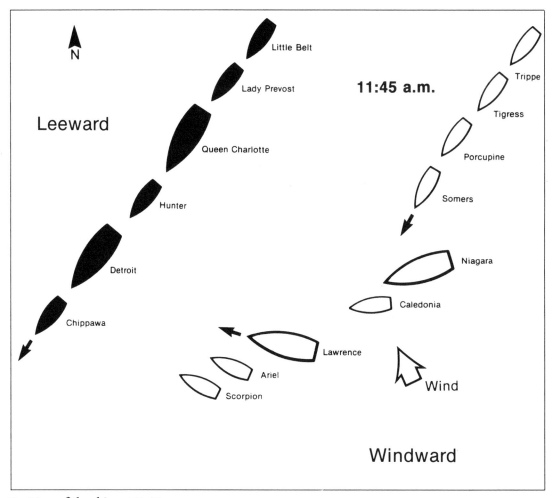

Position of the ships at 11:45 a.m.

the forward bulwark of the *Lawrence*, sending jagged splinters across the deck. It was followed with the first American reply as twenty-four-year-old Stephen Champlin called for *Scorpion*'s long 32-pounder to be fired. The *Scorpion* and *Ariel* had moved up to a station just ahead of the larboard bow of the *Lawrence*, which itself entered the bombardment at 11:55 a.m. with shots from its two 12-pound cannons; the port bow chaser gun had been moved over to the starboard side during the hour prior to the start of the fighting. After this preliminary exchange of shots, the action became general as all the vessels began to fire at various rates at the opponents to which they had been assigned.

This opening stage of the battle saw Perry struggling to manoeuvre the *Lawrence* into close quarters with the *Detroit*, so that the full impact of his battery of carronades could be inflicted upon the British. As he closed on Barclay's flagship he kept his two 12-pounders busy, but they offered little opposition to the hail of iron that was being thrown at the *Lawrence* from the British line. That fire, the strongest aspect of the British gunnery, began

96

Sharpshooters in the tops of the *Niagara* sniped at the British crews.

to take effect as the round shot blasted through the American bulwarks, tearing men apart, slashing the gun crews with knife-sharp splinters of wood, crushing them beneath overturned carronades and under the rigging that had been ripped from above. Perry ordered that the ships following him be signalled by means of a speaking trumpet to get in close to the enemy.

Master's Mate John Campbell had the crew of the *Chippawa* popping away with its little 9-pounder at the *Lawrence*. Champlin in the *Scorpion* and Packet in the *Ariel* kept their batteries blazing at the *Detroit*, but made the error of overloading their guns. On board the *Scorpion* a cannon blew off its mounts and fell into a hatchway. Also on that schooner, Midshipman John Clarke was killed by a round shot. Another gun, this time aboard the *Ariel*, burst wounding some of its crew. Perry ordered his tillermen to bring the *Lawrence*'s bow more towards the wind, so that he could try the range with his carronades. Slowly the brig turned toward the left. The starboard battery fired, but the shells fell short. Again, the helm was put down, and the brig was brought back on the course that angled towards the *Detroit*. A second time Perry called for his vessel to be yawed, but again the broadside proved ineffective. At about 12:20 p.m. the *Lawrence* was pulled in line parallel with the British once more and took up a station opposite the *General Hunter* at a distance that First Lieutenant Yarnell later judged to be about 225 metres. The full weight of her starboard carronades was divided among the ships in the British line. In Yarnell's words, "Our first division [the carronades on the forward part of the starboard side] was fought against the *Detroit* and our second against the *Queen Charlotte*, occasionally directed guns at the *Hunter*."[3]

Meanwhile, at the rear of the American line, the three schooners and the sloop *Trippe* were throwing their 24- and 32-pound balls at the *Little Belt* and the *Lady Prevost*. This shelling was taking place at well over 1,000 metres, a range at which Lieutenant Buchan's carronades were totally ineffective, leaving his crews open to a killing fire without the opportunity to respond.

In between the action at the two ends of the lines a curious series of events was beginning to develop. According to Perry's in-transit revision of the line of battle, Jesse Elliott had steered the *Niagara* to follow after the *Caledonia*, which would stay between the twin brigs. As the action commenced, Perry signalled the commanders of his squadron to engage the ships identified beforehand as their opponents. By 12:30, most of the American commanders had done just that, although Perry himself, totally involved in a tremendous cannonade with the main strength of the British line and assisted by the *Ariel* and *Scorpion*, was most closely engaged. The *Niagara*, however, was still well out of the fight. Elliott had not brought his brig down to run opposite the *Queen Charlotte* as planned. Instead, he maintained his station behind the *Caledonia* using his two 12-pound long guns to lob shots at his adversary. To Robert Barclay's eye, the *Niagara* "kept so far to Windward as to render the *Queen Charlotte*'s 24 Pounder Carronades useless."[4] Thomas Stokoe, executive officer aboard the *Queen Charlotte*, supported this view of events. A year later, at Barclay's court martial, he recalled that the *Caledonia*'s long guns, fired from a considerable distance had more effect than the long guns of the *Niagara*.[5] Aboard the *Lawrence* Lieutenant John Yarnell agreed with these estimates, putting Elliott's brig just more than one kilometre astern of the *Lawrence*.[6] At that distance, Elliott followed so closely behind *Caledonia* that at one point the *Niagara*'s main topsail had to be backed in order to prevent a collision with the more sluggishly sailing *Caledonia*. Yarnell remembered seeing the sail laying back against the mast; indeed the same procedure was being used to keep the *Lawrence* in the centre of the fight.

In opposition to the distant *Niagara* and the *Caledonia*, the *Queen Charlotte* was answering with its two long 12-pounders. Aboard the *Queen Charlotte* the expectation had been that the second American brig would close in fast and hard, but this was not happening. And just as well, because Lieutenant Thomas Stokoe had suddenly found himself in charge of the second British corvette. Tragically, in the first minutes of the fight, a round shot from either the *Niagara* or the *Caledonia* had come whistling aboard, simultaneously killing Commander Robert Finnis and the ranking officer of the Royal Newfoundland Regiment, Lieutenant James Garden, "mingling the blood of the one and the brains of the other, on the bulwark, in one melancholy and undistinguishable mass."[7] It was a decisive point in the combat, as Robert Barclay later stated, "Too soon, alas, was I deprived of the Services of the Noble and intrepid Captain Finnis . . . with him fell my greatest Support."[8]

Taking control of the situation, Thomas Stokoe waited for the *Niagara* to move in on his ship. When this did not happen Stokoe ordered more sail to be set and promptly passed to the port side of the *General Hunter* leapfrogging in line to support the *Detroit*, which was very heavily engaged. At about this time, more than an hour into the battle, Stokoe himself fell to the deck, wounded severely by a large splinter. As the first lieutenant was taken below, the command of the *Queen Charlotte* devolved to Provincial Marine Lieutenant Robert Irvine.

The second hour of the battle wore on and the casualties on board the *Detroit* and the *Lawrence* began to mount. A disproportionate number of the seamen aboard the British corvette were falling compared to the soldiers in the crew. Robert Barclay was thrown off his feet by a musket ball or a piece of wreckage that tore a gash in his thigh. He went below for medical attention from surgeon George Young, but soon returned to the deck. The *Detroit* was being ripped apart by the broadsides of the *Lawrence*. The rigging and sails were hanging in shreds, the bulwarks pierced by the 32-pound balls that had crashed through them. The crews of the guns were losing man after man as cannister and splinters mowed them down. Marines posted in the toptrees of the brig's masts were picking off the unsheltered British, whose blood was beginning to smear the sanded deck. Purser Hoffmenster, who had volunteered to join a gun crew, crumpled screaming to the deck, his knee torn apart. Able Seaman Daniel Mead and John Barnes, a landsman, were killed outright.

Aboard the *Lawrence*, the slaughter was just as nightmarish. His luck holding out, Perry strode his deck unharmed while all around him others were falling. A splinter knocked

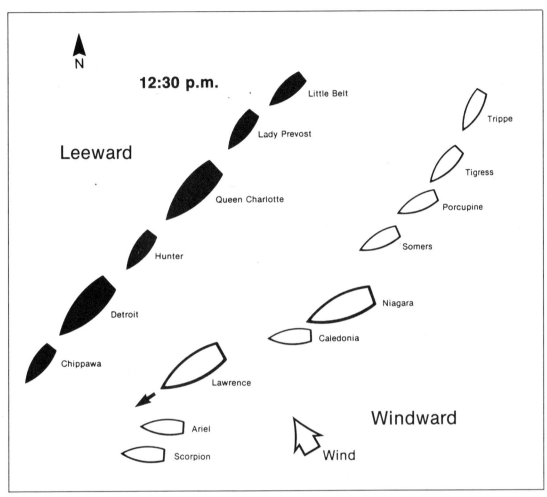

Position of the ships at 12:30 p.m.

young James Perry on his back, but the lad was soon up again. Second Lieutenant Dulaney Forrest, one of the men sent from the *Constitution*, was struck by a musket ball and collapsed, stunned. Seeing that Forrest was only winded, Perry helped him to his feet, whereupon the lieutenant cooly picked the ball out from where it had been tangled in his coat and put it in his pocket. Many others were less fortunate than these two officers, and along the deck of the *Lawrence* the dead and wounded began to pile up. Commandant Perry walked to the skylight and called below to the surgeon's assistant, Usher Parsons, to send up one of the attendants who had been assigned to help him.

Below deck Parsons was immersed in a hell of his own. With no sedatives, no concern for septic conditions and wielding a gruesome set of tools more typical of a shoemaker than a doctor, Parsons ministered to the wounded and dying. Splinters were picked out of gaping wounds, which were then roughly sutured together. Arteries pulsing blood were clamped off with tourniquets and fractured bones hastily set and splinted. Where such techniques offered

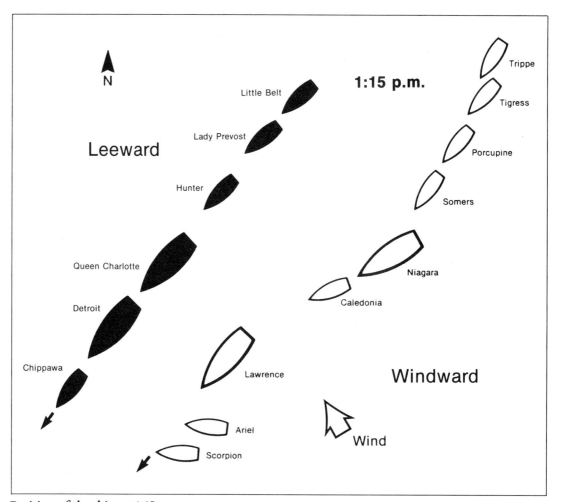

Position of the ships at 1:15 p.m.

no help, Parson's assistants seized the seamen while the doctor sliced through flesh with scissors and knives and then completed amputation with a saw. Less dangerous scrapes were bandaged and the patient sent back to his station. For some, however, there was no salvation. Lieutenant John Brooks, one of the marine officers serving aboard, was stricken by a cannon ball that tore into his upper leg, destroying his hip joint. Screaming in agony, he was carried below where Parsons could do little more than cover his ghastly wound and assure him that the end would not be long in coming. Brooks expired just before the close of the battle.

Somehow in this madhouse the men found reason for mirth. One of the three wounds that John Yarnell received was a jagged gash to his scalp. As he descended into Parson's operating theatre, he passed through a cloud of stuffing that had been ripped from a bank of hammocks. The feather-like stuffing stuck to the blood of his wound, forming a mantle around his head and causing the wounded to roar "out with laughter that the devil had come."[9]

The pivot-mounted gun on the *Detroit* is evident on the forecastle in Julian O. Davidson's painting.

Parsons had more than just the wounded and dying to worry about. Usually the place in warships that was alloted for a surgeon's grisly work was the cockpit, a portion of one of the lower decks well below the water line of the vessel. The *Lawrence* did not offer this sanctuary. Since it drew just less than three metres of water, the operating theatre was positioned above the water line in the officer's wardroom. As a result, no fewer than six cannon balls crashed through the hull and into the tiny space Parsons occupied. They too took their toll. "When the battle was raging most severely," Parsons recalled, "Midshipman Laub came down with his arm badly fractured; I applied a splint and requested him to go forward and lie down; as he was leaving me, and while my hand was on him, a cannon-ball struck him in the side, and dashed him against the other side of the room, which instantly terminated his sufferings."[10]

The action continued on toward 2:00 p.m. The schooners at the rear of the American line were gradually catching up and simultaneously having effect on the *Lady Prevost* and the *General Hunter.* Lieutenant George Bignell, newly appointed commander of the *Hunter,* was severely wounded and fell, followed shortly after by his second in command, Master's Mate Henry Gateshill. What little impact the weak batteries of the small brig could have on the distant enemy was further reduced with the loss of its officers. The *Lady Prevost* had also suffered badly and began to fall out of the line, drifting to the right of the corvettes, its rudder disabled. On board eight crew members were killed, nineteen wounded. Among the casualties were the severely injured Frederic Rolette and Lieutenant Edward Buchan, shot through the face. Only the *Little Belt* was escaping the kind of lethal drubbing that had already stripped three of the British ships of their commanding officers. The little sloop began to head toward the leeward side of the bigger ships.[11]

The two squadrons continued to crawl along in a southwesterly direction beneath a massive pall of smoke. The cannonade at the centre of the action had not let up for nearly two hours, but was becoming less regular. The murderous exchange of round shot, cannister and grape was sweeping the decks of men and dismantling the guns their mates were left to handle. Aboard the *Queen Charlotte* Seamen Jones, Tadley and Willsbrook joined their captain in death. Three of the late James Garden's Royal Newfoundlanders were killed, seven men of the 41st Regiment died, the eventual death toll on the *Queen Charlotte* rising to eighteen. On the *Detroit* the cost was no less grim. The number of wounded was approaching three dozen. Commander Barclay still held the deck, but his situation was precarious. First Lieutenant John Garland was cut down with a wound that left him dying, as was Master's Mate Thomas Clarke.

In spite of the murderous cost the fighting had taken, victory seemed faintly within the grasp of the British at that point. Their chief opponent, the *Lawrence*, was beginning to wither and was seen to fall back away from the *Detroit*. Perry's sailing master, William Taylor, explained the appearance of his ship as "presenting a picture too horrid for description—nearly the whole crew and officers and all prostrated on the deck, intermingled with broken spars, riggings, sails and in fact one confused heap of horrid ruins. Some of the guns were dismounted and mounted five times in action—some of these guns were mann'd three different times in action."[12] The number of killed and wounded was surpassing eighty. Somehow, Oliver Hazard Perry was escaping injury of any sort. Just before 2:30, together with the chaplain and the purser, Perry fired a shot from the last of the *Lawrence*'s starboard carronades and then told Yarnell that he had resolved to give up his flagship and to head for the *Niagara*. A shot-pierced boat that had been towed behind the brig was pulled along the port side of the ship. Perry quickly changed out of the plain sailor's jacket he had worn since the fighting began and put on his uniform coat. The flag, bearing "Don't Give Up The Ship," was hauled down and the young commandant stepped into the boat, which struck out for the *Niagara*. Standing in the stern, in full view of the British sharpshooters, Perry defiantly held his battle flag, until he was begged by his boat crew to sit down.

As Perry drew away from the *Lawrence*, Yarnell called for the Stars and Stripes to be lowered. Rather than take any more beating, the lieutenant was resolved to surrender. Aboard the *Detroit* the sign of surrender was not missed, but no ship's boat had survived the cannonade and there were scarcely enough men left to be spared for taking possession of the American flagship. Perry's departure from the *Lawrence* was clearly visible from the deck of the *Detroit*, and the British marksmen sniped at him. Also seen was the more ominous movement of the *Niagara* as it set more canvas in order to close on the faltering *Lawrence*. Robert Barclay saw that "the *Niagara* . . . was at this time perfectly fresh."[13] The *Detroit* was in a "very defenceless state . . . a perfect Wreck"[14] and support from the other ships in the squadron was weak at most. As he watched Perry's boat being rowed to the *Niagara*, the British commander probably wondered how he was going to handle the imminent attack of the enemy's second brig. The situation must have looked very dark, but it suddenly got darker. From some direction, perhaps from the *Scorpion* or *Ariel*, which had faithfully maintained their stations throughout the fray, came another salvo of cannister or round shot. Again the *Detroit* absorbed the blow, but some part of that blast tore into Robert Barclay's back ripping his right shoulder blade asunder. He was carried below, his authority passing to Second Lieutenant George Inglis and his subordinate Francis Purvis.

Little time was lost in Perry's transfer to the *Niagara*. That ship had been the object of some questions as the heat of the battle had risen. Usher Parsons observed that Jesse Elliott's ship "did not make sail when the *Lawrence* did, but hung back for two hours, when she should have followed the example of the *Lawrence*, and grappled with the *Queen Charlotte*."[15] The men on the flagship had been dismayed by this lack of support. "I expressed my surprise that the *Niagara* was not brought into close action," recalled John Yarnell. "The crew also expressed their surprise, but were encouraged by the officers to fight on till she should come down and take part with us."[16] The exact distance at which the *Niagara* held station is difficult to pin down. Perry's crew felt more effort could have been made by their cohorts to render them some support. On board the *Niagara* men felt that no inappropriate

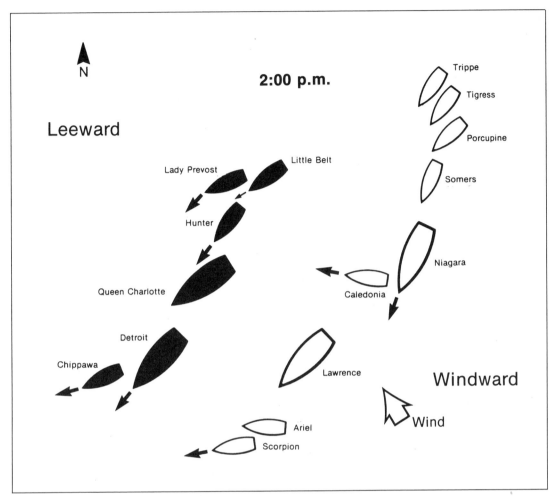

Position of the ships at 2:00 p.m.

hesitation had been allowed. "The lightness of the wind prevented our getting as close to the *Lawrence* as it was supposed, we intended," explained Midshipman Montgomery of the *Niagara*.[17] Elliott's own explanation was that the line of battle, once dictated, is an order that "no captain has a right to change, without authority, or a signal from the commanding vessel."[18] Breaking out of that line, as he did after 2:00 pm, he perceived to be at risk to his own head. Furthermore, Elliott later asked Perry why he had taken position opposite the *Hunter*, rather than moving further up so that the following ships could take their places. Elliott apparently did not question Lieutenant Stokoe's moving the *Queen Charlotte* past the *Hunter* in order to lend more support to his flagship, nor did he take it as an example of what he could do. Instead, for more than two hours Elliott kept the *Niagara* so distant from the main action that in the warships on both sides of the fight, and especially aboard the *Lawrence,* men viewed his conduct with doubt.

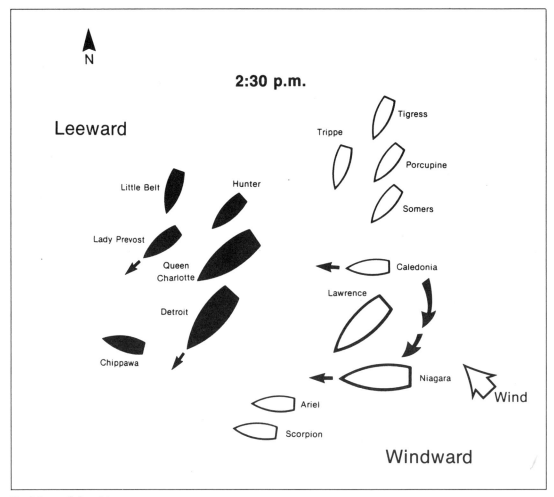

2:30 p.m.

Position of the ships at 2:30 p.m.

When he decided to make his move, Jesse Elliott hailed Lieutenant Daniel Turner of the *Caledonia* to bear up, which Turner did, setting more sail to move out of Elliott's way and to get in closer to the enemy. The *Niagara* let fall its foresail and cruised down toward the head of the British line. Elliott did not select a direct route for charging at the *Detroit*, however. From the *Scorpion* Stephen Champlin saw the *Niagara* range "ahead of the *Lawrence*, and to windward of her, thus bringing the commodore's ship between her and the enemy, when she might have passed to leeward and relieved the *Lawrence* from the destructive fire of the enemy."[19] The breeze, during this time, had freshened and most of the ships began to move at a faster pace toward the southwest, while the *Lawrence* with its sails and rigging cut to shreds, fell behind, "lying like a log upon the water."[20]

It was during this move to pass around on the windward of the wrecked flagship that Commandant Perry's boat intercepted the *Niagara*. He hurried up the side of the brig and was

Perry shifted his flag from the *Lawrence* to the *Niagara* at the height of the action. This is one of several dramatized versions of the event.

met by Elliott. The two were seen to shake hands and exchange words, after which Elliott himself got into Perry's boat and directed it to be rowed toward the schooners in the rear of the squadron. Perry had ordered him to speed them on, while he planned to steer the *Niagara* through the British line.

Perry found the *Niagara* to be in very good order, further evidence of its lack of involvement in the battle that had started nearly three hours before. Some damage had been inflicted upon the rigging, including the cutting of backstays and shrouds. Two men had been killed, several wounded. The vessel was quite manageable, however, and continued the

The *Queen Charlotte* drew up under the lee of the *Detroit*, as the *Niagara* bore down on the British line. ▶

As the *Queen Charlotte* and *Detroit* lay entwined and immobile, the *Niagara* delivered its devastating broadside.

sweep that brought the *Niagara* bearing down upon the British. Perry steered to pass across the bow of the *Detroit*.

Aboard the British flagship George Inglis watched the Americans approach and felt the effect of the mighty blast of its starboard carronades. The order in the British line of battle had been completely lost. With a steadier breeze the schooner *Lady Prevost* had wallowed past the *Detroit* and was now close to the tiny *Chippawa*. The *Queen Charlotte* was ranging up

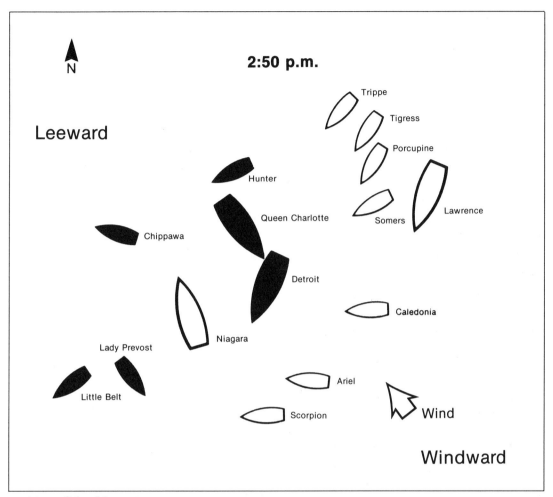

2:50 p.m.

Position of the ships at 2:50 p.m.

near the *Detroit*'s stern, aiming to pass on that ship's starboard side. Further back was the *Hunter*, while the *Little Belt* was making way towards the west. Urged on by Elliott, the American schooners had put out their sweeps and begun the strenuous task of rowing their vessels to bring them up to the British as fast as possible.

Inglis decided that his best strategy would be to get his starboard battery into action. It had stood unused all afternoon, though not undamaged, and could at least offer some fresh resistance to the oncoming *Niagara*. Inglis passed the order to bring the bow of the *Detroit* across the wind. Among the tattered rigging the survivors of his crew fought to turn the wounded corvette. Halfway through the procedure, as the wind pressed the sails against the mast, pushing the ship itself into reverse, cries of alarm rang out and the *Detroit* rammed backwards into *Queen Charlotte*'s larboard side, their spars tangling. With its starboard battery still ineffective the *Detroit* lay impotent in the water, as Perry's *Niagara* crossed in front of it raking it from stem to stern with a deadly cannonade.

A panoramic view of the battle of Lake Erie

As the hour of three approached, the climactic moments of the battle for control of Lake Erie were played out. The *Niagara* broke through the British line, its well-crewed batteries on both sides of the ship blazing away at a range of less than one hundred metres. To larboard the *Chippawa* and the *Lady Prevost* received the full force of the unscathed carronades. Only five casualties had accumulated on the smaller of the two schooners, among them the *Chippawa*'s commander, Master's Mate John Campbell, wounded slightly. The deck of the *Lady Prevost* was empty, however, all the men having run below. Deserted, Lieutenant Edward Buchan could be seen hanging over the rail, screaming in torment from his horrible wound. Perry saw this pathetic sight and ordered his larboard guns silenced.

Meanwhile, the starboard carronades of the *Niagara* continued to pound the two British corvettes. The Royal Ensign, flapping in the rigging of the *Queen Charlotte*, came down in defeat. On the *Detroit* Inglis had managed to break free of the *Queen*, but could get no more control of his ship. "Laying completely unmanageable, every Brace cut away, the Mizen Topmast, and Gaff down, all the other Masts badly Wounded, not a stay left forward, Hull shattered very much, a number of the Guns disabled, and the Enemys Squadron Raking both Ships, a head and astern, none of our own in a situation to support us, I was under the painful necessity," Inglis explained, "of answering the Enemy to say we had struck."[21] Since the Royal Ensign had been nailed to the mast, Inglis ordered one of the survivors to tie a white cloth to a boarding pike and wave it back and forth to indicate his surrender.

As the guns were stilled, the *Chippawa* and the *Little Belt* attempted to escape by fleeing to leeward. But the *Trippe*, which had come up ahead of the other schooners, pursued the *Chippawa*; the *Scorpion* went after the *Little Belt*. In time, after being fired at, the British vessels hauled down their flags. The battle ended and a silence fell over the intermingled cluster of British and American warships; a silence broken by some cheers of victory and many cries of men wounded and dying.

Jesse Elliott had boarded the schooner *Somers* and taken over command of its forward gun. When the surrender had been signalled, the aft gunner wanted to take one last shot at the British. Elliott berated him for so cowardly an act, but the man roared back that the British had pressed him into service nine times and he wanted revenge. The cannons remained silent and Elliott was rowed over to the ravaged *Detroit*. There he found a scene that provoked this anecdote years later:

> I went on board the *Detroit*, to take possession, and such was the quantity of blood on the deck, that in crossing it, my feet slipped from under me, and I fell; my clothing becoming completely saturated and covered with gore! I went below to see Capt. Barclay, who tendered me his sword; but I refused it, and anticipated the wishes of Capt. Perry, by assuring him that every kindness would be shown himself and the other prisoners.[22]

At 4:00 Oliver Hazard Perry returned to the shattered *Lawrence*. His surviving comrades met him at the gangway, but the violent nature of their experience left them mute. As Usher Parsons remembered, "The battle was won and he was safe, but the deck was slippery with blood, and strewn with the bodies of twenty officers and men, some of whom had set at table with us at our last meal, and the ship resounded everywhere with the groans of the wounded."[23] Perry went to his cabin where he penned a quick message to General Harrison and, in so doing, created one of his own memorials: "We have met the enemy and they are ours — Two Ships, two Brigs, one Schooner and one Sloop."[24]

Soon the surviving senior officers from each of the British vessels arrived at the *Lawrence* to tender their formal surrenders. Robert Barclay sent Lieutenant O'Keefe of the 41st Regiment to represent him. O'Keefe appeared in full dress and, despite Elliott's comment, offered Barclay's sword to the conquering Perry. Commandant Perry, accepted the surrender, but bade O'Keefe and the others to keep their weapons. Later, he went over to see Barclay in person and found him dangerously wounded and despondent.

As evening approached the vessels were anchored, their position now near Western Sister Island. Guards were organized to secure the British prisoners. Work details hustled to repair torn rigging and to splint damaged masts and spars. It was decided that a prompt burial was the best way to deal with the dead, except for the fallen officers, who would be buried ashore. Accordingly, each man who had lost his life during the battle was sewn into his hammock with a cannonball at his feet. With the rights of an Episcopal Service read over them, the dead were committed one by one to the deep.

As most men collapsed from exhaustion, the last little drama of the day was played out. After a long chase, Stephen Champlin's *Scorpion* returned with the *Little Belt* in tow and anchored under the stern of the *Niagara*, just as the ship's bell struck midnight.

10
"THIS VICTORY, SO DECISIVE AND IMPORTANT"

THE SUN BURNED off the mist hanging over the western reach of Lake Erie on Saturday, September 11, 1813 and revealed the ships of Perry's squadron at anchor hovering over their six British prizes. After months of frantic activity the contest for control of Lake Erie had been settled in a single spectacular clash of men and ships. The severity of that conflict was painfully obvious as the survivors sailed labouriously back to the anchorage at Put-in-Bay.

Residents on South Bass Island gazed in awe at the veritable wrecks, which had carried the flags of the two squadrons proudly into battle. The *Lawrence* was devastated and "the *Detroit* and *Queen Charlotte* were shattered from bow to stern; on their larboard side there was hardly a hand's breadth free from the dent of a shot. Balls, cannister and grape were found lodged in their bulwarks."[1]

The lists of casualties painted a statistical picture that resembled the horrific conditions of the flagships. On five of the British ships the commanding officers had been either killed or wounded; on four of those vessels a similar fate had befallen the seconds in command. Although eight American officers had been wounded and three killed, none of them was in command of a vessel, half of them were midshipmen. The tally of casualties clearly confirmed which ships had been in the centre of the action. The *Lawrence* stood out, having lost nearly two thirds of its crew to injury and death; that same fraction represented the flagship's portion of the total American loss. On the *Detroit* and the *Queen Charlotte* one man in three had been killed or wounded. The *Lady Prevost* suffered similarly, while

aboard the smaller vessels on the periphery of the action, the toll of death and dismemberment was proportionately light.

VESSELS	WOUNDED		KILLED		TOTALS
BRITISH	Officers	Men	Officers	Men	
Detroit	2	39	1	10	52
Queen Charlotte	2	22	2	16	42
Lady Prevost	2	18	–	8	28
General Hunter	2	3	–	3	8
Chippawa	1	3	–	1	5
Little Belt	–	–	–	–	–
TOTALS	9	85	3	38	135
AMERICAN					
Lawrence	6	55	2	20	83
Niagara	2	23	–	2	27
Caledonia	–	3	–	–	3
Ariel	–	3	–	1	4
Scorpion	–	–	1	1	2
Somers	–	2	–	–	2
Trippe	–	2	–	–	2
Others	–	–	–	–	–
TOTALS	8	88	3	24	123

A comparison of casualties received on board the British and American fleets during the battle.

Sunday morning was set aside for the combined funeral service for the officers killed in the squadrons. With great civility the survivors on each side arranged a service that saw a cortege of ships' boats carry the bodies of the three British officers Robert Finnis, John Garland and James Garden and the three Americans John Brooks, Henry Laub and John Clarke to the tree-covered site on the shore of South Bass Island that had been chosen for a communal grave. In a double line, the men of the squadrons formed a procession on land and carried the fallen officers to their resting place. One version of the event noted that "the hero of Erie, stood there, supporting with his arm the wounded and shattered figure of Commodore Barclay, who leaned heavily against him."[2] An Anglican service was held at the graveside and the dead were interred "English and American side by side, undistinguished."[3] Later in the day, the skies darkened and a gale roared across the Bass Islands. The battered ships tugged at their anchors, the *Detroit* and *Queen Charlotte* wallowing so violently that their fractured masts crashed overboard.

113

The funeral procession of the American and British officers

Sunday the twelfth was also the day for the preparation of reports. Perry wrote to Secretary of the Navy William Jones in a proper professional style devoid of any spectacular descriptions of the gruesome fighting.[4] He mentioned the names of men he had seen behave admirably and offered suitable memorials for the dead officers. Of the actions of the *Niagara* no directly critical statement was made. Instead, Perry mentioned that "at half past two, the wind springing up, Captain Elliott was enabled to bring his vessel . . . gallantly into action . . . the *Niagara* being very little injured." Of Elliott's conduct Perry assured the secretary that during the battle he "evinced his characteristic bravery . . . and, since the close of the action, has given me the most able and essential assistance." These carefully chosen words would come back to haunt the commandant.

Robert Barclay's report, dictated the same day, also contained little evidence of the bloody combat.[5] Like Perry, he lauded some of his men and mourned the loss of his officers and friends. Opposite to the style of Perry's account, Barclay minced no words in blaming the disastrous results of the battle squarely upon "the many disadvantages" under which he had

114

suffered and which his repeated requests to his superiors during the summer had done little to relieve. He also cited the loss of the wind gauge, the incapacitation of his officers and the inadequacies of his crews as reasons for the defeat. His despatch closed with a statement of his belief that "under such circumstances the Honor of His Majesty's Flag has not been tarnished."

With the dead buried and the records written, attention was turned to the survivors of the battle. The *Lawrence* was converted into a hospital ship, hastily mended, and sent back to Erie on September 18 under the command of John Yarnell. Usher Parsons and a British

As a prisoner, Provincial Lieutenant Robert Irvine of the *Queen Charlotte* sketched (left to right) his former ship, the *Niagara*, the *Detroit*, and the *Lawrence* at anchor at Put-in-Bay.

General Harrison greeted by the women of Amherstburg. A romanticized version of the villagers who remained in Amherstburg to meet the invading army.

doctor named Kennedy cared for the infirm, losing only two patients before the vessel arrived at Erie on the twenty-third. Robert Barclay, whose injuries appeared to be life threatening at first, and the other wounded British officers remained aboard the *Detroit* and *Queen Charlotte.* A surgeon named Robert Richardson, who had been attached to the Provincial Marine, remained to care for Barclay, assisted quite likely by George Young.[6] To Perry, Barclay had expressed his fear that staying in the area of western Lake Erie would bring on his death. The American commandant responded by putting the wheels in motion to effect Barclay's repatriation at the earliest possible date.

More than three hundred of the British were well enough to stand the rigours of imprisonment. They temporarily came under the care of Jesse Elliott who had been placed in charge of corralling the prisoners and preparing them for transportation. On September 15 and 16 sixty-four men from the Royal Newfoundland Regiment, 119 from the 41st and 125 seamen from the Royal Navy and the Provincial Marine were shipped to Sandusky, Ohio. From there, they set out on a march to Frankfort, Kentucky, where they were detained for the better part of a year. The months of incarceration and the weary trek back to Lake Erie during the late summer of 1814 added to the scars earned in the battle; the men returned to Canada haggard and ill, some of them disabled for life.[7]

With the barrier posed by the British squadron eliminated, an invasion of the Detroit frontier needed only final organization to be made into a reality. On September 19 Perry, who had been officially confirmed as a post captain in Washington on the day of the battle and could now be legitimately referred to as commodore, sailed to Sandusky in the *Ariel* to confer with General Harrison. The two commanders wasted no time in taking action. Harrison's army was ferried to Put-in-Bay and from there to Middle Sister Island. This movement was completed by September 26, and the following day 4,500 troops embarked in the ships of the American squadron plus the *Little Belt, Chippawa, Hunter* and *Lady Prevost* and a host of small boats. The invasion force landed on the beach twenty kilometres from Amherstburg fully expecting a fusillade of musketry to hail down upon them, but their apprehension was unwarranted. No one was there to oppose them.

For Henry Procter, the days since Barclay had weighed anchor and sailed out to meet the Americans had been filled with considerable anguish. The battle had been observed from a point down the shore from Amherstburg. The billows of smoke surrounding the vessels, which appeared like specks in the lenses of the watchers' telescopes, left the impression that the day had been won. But time proved the painful opposite result. Procter, on the twelfth wrote to De Rottenburg, "The Wind was fair for Amherstburg the whole on the 10th and the 11th . . . and on the latter Day the vessels evidently under one Flag worked down the Lake."[8] He rambled on in his letter about defensive steps to take, the difficulty of his position and his intention to retreat.

Almost a week later the British retreat was far from organized. Procter had ordered the dismantling of Fort Malden, but had kept his other intentions more or less to himself. Tecumseh and the Indians were menacing, eager to fight the Americans, unsure of what Procter was going to do next. At one point Procter met with the Indians and listened to a passionate speech from Tecumseh, in which the chief is reputed to have cried, "Father—Listen! Our fleet has gone out; we know they have fought; we heard the great guns; but know nothing of what has happened to our father with the one arm."[9] On September 18 Procter formally announced his plans to retreat. The citizenry was urged to pack up its belongings and join the trek toward Sandwich. The public buildings in the naval yard and the fort were put to the torch on September 23, while an unwieldy train of wagons full of people and possessions straggled out of town. The fort at Detroit was burned and the troops moved back across the river to Sandwich on the twenty-seventh. A course was set to follow the southern shore of Lake St. Clair to the mouth of the Thames River. With families and their baggage going ahead, Procter led his 450 men almost forty kilometres up the Thames to Moravian-town, where on October 5 a stand was made against the American invaders.

Since landing on September 27, the Americans had advanced rapidly by land, while Perry and Elliott proceeded in some of their vessels to Lake St. Clair. The *Scorpion, Tigress* and *Porcupine* entered the Thames in pursuit of the two gunboats that Procter was using to transport his munitions. The British situation was quickly disintegrating, since Procter had failed to keep close control of his retreat or make preparations for a rear action. Some Indians offered a cessation of hostilities to Harrison, which was accepted. The victory for the Americans came on October 5 when Procter's army, supported by militia and the remaining Indians, was overwhelmed and routed at Moraviantown. Six hundred men were captured. Tecumseh was killed. Procter fled towards Lake Ontario with a fraction of his former force.

Before returning to Put-in-Bay, Harrison and Perry issued a proclamation ensuring the inhabitants that their homes and families would be secure from further depredations. According to one observer, sick of the hordes of Indians and martial law, the local townspeo-ple "particularly those of Malden were pleased with the change."[10] General Lewis Cass was placed in charge of both sides of the Detroit River.

More than a week before Procter's army collapsed at Moraviantown, the bitter news of Barclay's loss filtered through to George Prevost and James Yeo. When the verbal accounts were confirmed by the publication of Commodore Perry's report, Yeo wrote to Admiral Warren at Halifax and formally announced the defeat.[11] Yeo explained that he was "per-fectly uninformed as to Captain Barclay's reasons for risking an action before his reinforce-ment of seamen arrived, which was well on their way at the time of the action." He repeated a rumour that pinned a good deal of the blame on Henry Procter for ordering the squadron to sail. The commodore was sure, however, that if Procter and Barclay had only waited a short time, there would not have been "any serious consequences to the garrison." Yeo ended the letter with a firm statement of belief that "Captain Barclay did not hesitate a moment, but heroically devoted himself and the squadron to . . . the honour of the British flag." At that point, it was thought that the naval commander might have died from his wounds.

This reaction to the defeat was echoed by a general order from Prevost's headquarters in Montreal, dated November 24, that dealt with the losses on the Right Division.[12] The first half of the memorandum was a scathing criticism of the conduct of Henry Procter in his retreat and battle at Moraviantown and featured such rebukes as, "It is with poignant grief and mortification that He [the governor general] now beholds its [the army of the Right Division] well earned Laurels tarnished, and its conduct calling loudly for reproach and censure." Barclay's official report had reached headquarters by this time and must have impressed Prevost, since the second portion of the lengthy document praised the bravery and determination of his efforts: "Captain Barclay and his brave Crew have, by their gallant daring, and self devotion to their Country's cause, preserved its honor and their own, even in defeat."

When Commodore Yeo finally received Barclay's own version of the battle (containing his blunt explanations for the outcome of the battle) he wrote a second letter to Admiral Warren.[13] This one was less laudatory of the defeated commander and failed to represent the facts as they had actually developed. "The honour of the British flag seems to have been nobly upheld," the commodore began, "I am of the opinion . . . that officer was not justified in seeking a contest, the results of which he almost foresaw must prove disastrous." Yeo

After Perry's defeat of Barclay, the American patriotic cartoonists had a field day.

recollected his view of events leading up to the defeat, clearly attempting to distance himself from any blame. After all, he "had written to that officer" informing him that reinforcements would be sent shortly. Barclay had responded on September 6 that he still did not have enough men and then, "giving a time of three days for men to reach him at a distance of three hundred miles," he set out to face the enemy. True, Yeo admitted, there was a shortage of flour at Amherstburg, but not of grain, which Procter had been forced to burn. Yeo neglected to mention that Procter's supplies officer had warned early in August the local mills were not operating, nor did he list the other shortages that had prompted Procter and Barclay's joint decision. Yeo ended his condemnation by declaring that the general should never have urged the commander "to so hazardous and unequal a contest."

In the United States the news of victory had been met with a surge of patriotic celebration. Candles were lit in the homes of those who could afford such a modest extravagance. The whole of New York's city hall was "illuminated" for the event. Dedications were voted to the brave sailors whose capture of an entire British squadron added gloriously to the string of unprecedented American victories in ship-to-ship actions with the British on the Atlantic. The Pennsylvania legislature presented a gold medal to the commodore and a silver medal to every man in the squadron. The federal congress voted a gold medal to be given to Perry *and* Elliott and silver medals to the relatives of fallen officers. Each midshipman and sailing master received a commemorative sword, while all commissioned officers were granted three months' extra pay. The captured British ships were bought by the government as prizes and this money divided among the victors. Perry and Elliott each received $7,140 (Congress voted the commodore $5,000 more.) Sailing masters and lieutenants earned nearly $3,000, while each sailor was given only $200. As senior officer on the lakes, Isaac Chauncey was given the biggest portion of the prize money $12,750, rather a nice reward for having been completely involved elsewhere.[14] Songs and poems were penned to memorialize the event, often poking fun at the British, as this verse did:

> On Erie's wave, while Barclay brave,
> With *Charlotte* making merry,
> He chanced to take the belly-ache,
> We drenched him so with *Perry*.[15]

Isaac Chauncey responded to the news of the victory with markedly restrained enthusiasm. Upon receipt of Perry's report, he commented that the "victory, so decisive and important in its consequences, reflects the highest honour upon the heroes that achieved it, and appears to be duly appreciated by your country."[16] The rest of the commodore's response dealt at length with what he felt Perry should do next to secure the upper lakes. Perhaps Chauncey's chagrin, caused by the lack of success he had attained on Lake Ontario, impeded his willingness to properly congratulate the glorious Perry.

It was an American newspaper that brought the first word of the battle to England. On November 8, Perry's hasty note to General Harrison appeared as an unexplained quote in the *Times* of London.[17] Four days later an account of the battle, based on Perry's official report printed in a Halifax newspaper, took up the better part of one column in the *Times*.[18] The editors acknowledged the loss of the squadron, but explained that the British ships had been "wholly manned and equipped by the inhabitants of the Province." Perry was sarcastically chastised for having "heroically quitted her [the *Lawrence*] in the midst of the engagement" and later allowing the flag of the yielding *Lawrence* to be raised again! The commodore, in the minds of the editors, could hardly be called "an officer, after the disgraceful conduct which he seems to have pursued." The action was described briefly with a modicum of accuracy and the British Naval Administration, whose efforts were considered to "have been on a scale of laudable magnitude," was declared exempt from blame for the loss. Of Robert Barclay and the others who had given their blood and their lives to hold the British line, not a single mention was made. For relatives of the Royal Navy officers in England the final weeks of 1813 must have been filled with despair, after the shocking news of the defeat combined with an absence from the *Times* of any further references to the battle in the weeks that followed.

Perry and Harrison's capture of the Right Division of the British provinces remained more or less uncontested until the end of the war. With the signing of the Treaty of Ghent on December 24, 1814, the boundary between Upper Canada and Michigan Territory was automatically redrawn down the Detroit River. Amherstburg, Fort Malden, Sandwich and the Thames were returned to the British, and people on both sides of the river picked up the pieces of their war-torn world. Veterans of the conflict must have shaken their heads at the senseless loss and disruption of so many young lives in pursuit of a goal that was relinquished so simply.

11
MEN AND SHIPS

COMMODORE PERRY, THE VICTOR of Put-in-Bay, as the lake battle became known, returned to the South Bass Island anchorage aboard the *Ariel* along with General Harrison on October 19. Also on board the schooner was a group of British officers from the 41st Regiment, lately captured at the fight near Moraviantown. When the *Ariel* had dropped anchor at Put-in-Bay they took advantage of the opportunity to visit the shattered corvette *Detroit* and to pay their respects to Robert Barclay. One of them later recalled:

> On being introduced in Captain Barclay's cabin, we found that gallant officer in bed, presenting a most helpless picture of mutilation. Pain and disappointment were upon his brow, and the ruddy hue of health, from which he had ever been remarkable, had deserted him. In short, of his former self there then seemed to be little left besides his untainted honor.[1]

Despite his weakened state, five and a half weeks of recuperation had allowed Robert Barclay to regain his health sufficiently to accept Oliver Perry's offer of immediate transportation to Presque Isle. Still painfully disabled and in need of constant aid, the British commander travelled with Harrison and Perry in the *Ariel*, accompanied by several of the other ships, to Erie, arriving there on October 22. The population of the town turned out in force to welcome their new heroes, a response that Perry would see repeated in other places. As Erie celebrated, though, Perry did not forget the sensibilities of his wounded companion, making sure that Robert Barclay was comfortably provided for with a lodging in the hotel he had used during the summer.

Rising over one hundred metres above South Bass Island, Perry's Victory and International Peace Memorial Tower commemorates the battle of Lake Erie and the friendship between the former antagonists. The structure was completed in 1915.

The next day the party sailed on to Buffalo where, during the final days of October, the two former adversaries parted company. Perry had arranged for Barclay's parole, which meant the commander was free to cross the Niagara River to British territory safely. With Barclay probably went several officers and men from the squadron who could continue to look after their incapacitated leader; among them may have been surgeon George Young from the *Detroit*. Before Barclay took his leave, he gave Perry the gift of a sextant as a token of thanks for the kindnesses that the American had shown him.

At Buffalo Oliver Hazard Perry also handed over command of the Upper Lakes squadron to Jesse Elliott. Perry had petitioned the navy secretary before the end of September for permission to resign his post on Lake Erie, a request which was promptly granted. That decision infuriated Isaac Chauncey who felt "the principle that it establishes will be found to be a troublesome one."[2] Chauncey needed experienced officers. He was worried that others would seek permission to leave the lakes and feared that Perry's speedy departure from Erie would leave bills, accrued by the shipbuilders, unpaid and left to sit on his desk at Sackets Harbour. This last concern was a valid one, for Perry did leave the post with things undone. In December Chauncey was still writing to the secretary about the lack of information he had received from his former subordinate.

Commodore Perry travelled homeward bathed in the light of his heroic accomplishments, leaving the lakes far behind him. He was soon to be assigned to the frigate *Java*, but that ship did not sail before the war ended, and so Perry missed the opportunity to have another go at humiliating the British.

Robert Barclay began his journey home also, but under circumstances far different from those of the American officer. He had lost an entire squadron of ships, a disaster that was virtually unheard of in the annals of Royal Navy history. True enough, there was no shortage of reasons for that loss, but for Barclay the days and weeks spent in returning to England must have been filled with anxiety over the treatment he could expect from his less than compassionate superiors at the Admiralty in London. To make matters worse, his injuries left him gravely disabled; various contemporary reports of the battle asserted that he had completely lost his remaining right arm. It is an indication of Barclay's robust constitution and determined outlook that he was able to cope with the agonies of his mind and survive the misery of his wounds. Exactly how he managed these feats is unknown. He crossed the Niagara River and returned to British territory in late October. He spent a portion of the winter convalescing at the home of Thomas Dickson in Queenston, where he dined with visiting military officers and was often seen walking in the town, his wounded right arm supported upon a board.[3] From Queenston Barclay made his way eventually to Kingston, before leaving for England. There is no record available of any meeting he held with Sir James Yeo or with Sir George Prevost to discuss the events that had occurred on the Right Division. Part of his remaining days in Canada were spent writing to people like Henry Procter and Robert Gilmor collecting from them confirmation of the grim situation at Amherstburg, which his own letter book (lost during or after the battle) would have described. He also penned a memo to George Prevost attesting to the significant roles played in the September 10 battle by several members of the Provincial Marine to whom he had not given sufficient credit in his official account of the battle.[4] Barclay did not leave the country at least until some time in June, since he received letters at Montreal from Gilmor and Procter during that time.[5]

According to the anecdotes of his family's history, Robert Barclay is reported to have written, during those troublesome days, to a young woman in Scotland named Agnes Cossar and informed her about his grievous misfortunes.[6] Apparently the two were engaged, and the naval commander was stoically resolved to free her of any promises that had passed between them. Perhaps during his brief visit in 1809 Barclay had met the fair Miss Cossar, and their correspondence over the years had led to a long-distance commitment. Whatever the nature of their relationship, family tradition has it that Agnes wrote back to her badly disabled fiancé and informed him that if there was enough left of the man to embody his soul that would be more than enough for her. There was at least something in the world for Robert Barclay to look forward to, and when he returned to Scotland he wasted no time in making Agnes Cossar his wife. Although the spectre of court martial hung over their heads, the young couple was honoured by an unexpected gift. The merchants of Quebec, in appreciation of Barclay's efforts on the lakes, presented him with two commemorative tureens worth one hundred guineas. Their value and the kind words in their inscriptions made them much-cherished treasures for the newlyweds.

On September 9, 1814 Commander Robert Heriot Barclay (his acting commission had been formally confirmed in England several weeks after the battle) reported on board HMS *Gladiator*, a 44-gun frigate, anchored at Portsmouth to appear before the court martial inquiring into his conduct and that of his officers and men during the loss of the Lake Erie squadron.[7] Residing as president of the court was Rear Admiral of the White Edward James Foote. Beside him at the conference table situated in the great cabin at the stern of the ship sat twelve captains from the fleet, ready to hear evidence and direct questions to Commander Barclay. The commander's sword was handed over to the court at the beginning of the hearing and laid upon the table. Spectators filled the spare seats in the cabin and watched the proceedings. The various articles of correspondence and reports were read, and Barclay gave a detailed verbal explanation of the circumstances that had preceded his loss. During that time, he openly challenged some of the comments made by his superior Commodore Yeo, who was not present. The witnesses, who included Thomas Stokoe, Francis Purvis and George Young, were next called in to testify. Then the court adjourned to render its decision.

Barclay did not have long to wait. He was recalled before the court of inquiry and found his sword positioned on the table so that the hilt faced him; in other words, he had been absolved of blame. The conclusions of the court were read aloud and declared that Barclay had suffered from inadequate support and had been left without an alternative but to fight. He, his officers and men, described as gallant and worthy of great praise, were "fully and honourably acquitted."[8] It was a grand moment for the one-armed Scot. A seemingly insurmountable burden had been lifted from his shoulders. The threat of public humiliation, and even execution, was erased, and he could look forward to a continuation of his career. Undoubtedly Commander and Mrs. Barclay joined with Stokoe and the others to celebrate their salvation from disgrace and to dream about a brighter tomorrow.

The Barclay court martial, despite its agreeable resolution, produced a couple of unexpected repercussions. One affected Barclay himself; the other his former adversaries. When it was reported in the newspapers that the Lake Erie squadron had been inadequately supported, there was a call in the House of Lords for the transcript of the court martial to be tabled so that the conduct of the government could be debated.[9] In response, members of the government defended their actions and suggested that the whole story would not be known until further documents reached England. By the time the matter was dropped in February of

1815, one voice had claimed that Barclay should never have gone out to fight with the odds so much against him. This political wrangling, combined with the post-war shortage of job opportunities, left Barclay high and dry without a command for the better part of a decade.

In the United States the publication of evidence given at the Barclay court martial added fuel to a fire that was leaving scorch marks on the heroes of Put-in-Bay. Assertions that the *Niagara* "kept so far to Windward as to render the *Queen Charlotte*'s . . . Carronades useless"[10] helped to confirm the hurtful gossip being spread about Jesse Elliott's hesitant handling of the second brig. The whispering about Elliott's conduct had begun immediately after the battle. A letter sent by William Taylor, sailing master of the *Lawrence*, to his brother epitomizes the manner in which the stories spread. "Why we suffered so much," Taylor wrote, "and the *Niagara* and several other vessels little or none will be a subject for your private ear."[11]

The rumours grew at Put-in-Bay and Jesse Elliott heard them. On September 18 he wrote to Perry declaring, "I am informed a report has been circulated by some malicious persons, prejudicial to my vessel when engaged with the enemy's fleet. I will thank you if you will with candor state to me the conduct of myself, officers and crew."[12] Perry responded with dubious-sounding reassurances. "I have no doubt," he wrote back, "had not the *Queen Charlotte* have ran from the *Niagara*, from the superior order I observed her in, you would have taken her in twenty minutes."[13] According to Usher Parsons, the commodore later openly regretted this letter, saying that he had written it in hope that the victory would not be sullied by accusations of negligence against Elliott.[14] There was no stopping the rumours, and when the Barclay court martial proceedings became public, the chastened Captain Elliott petitioned the Department of the Navy for a court martial inquiry into his conduct. The request was granted, and the court was held at Washington in April 1815. Over several days officers from the *Lawrence* and *Niagara* testified as to their perception of the events of September 10. The verdict set by the judges conferred upon Elliott a full exoneration, but the matter did not end there, as one party after another stoked up the debate and relations between Perry and Elliott soured.[15] In time they might have settled things on the duelling ground, had fate not had other plans.

Oliver Perry was not present at the court martial of his former second in command, since he had sailed for the Mediterranean as captain of the 44-gun frigate *Java*. He returned to the States and was given, in 1819, the *John Adams*, to take for a cruise in the West Indies. In August of that year, while in Venezuela, the hero of Lake Erie contracted yellow fever and died on the twenty-third, his birthday. His promising naval career cut short at age thirty-four, Perry was buried at Port of Spain, Trinidad. An appreciative public did not forget him and pushed for his remains to be returned to Rhode Island, where they were re-interred beneath a memorial obelisk at Newport in 1826.

Elliott outlived his commodore and eventually became, in 1835, the commander in chief of the Mediterranean Sea fleet. A joint protest by a group of his subordinate officers interrupted that term and caused him to be temporarily suspended from duty.[16] Over the years he continued to defend his actions on Lake Erie and experienced no shortage of support or criticism for his position. In 1845 Jesse Elliott died, leaving the Perry-Elliott controversy as a legacy that is still preserved today.

Prevost's reputation had faded badly by the war's end. After his premature death within a year of the conclusion of the war, friends and family spent years trying to clear his name of the failure attached to it.

The British had their share of scandal, as well. For his handling of things on the Right Division Henry Procter was bitterly criticized. A court martial held at Montreal, late in 1814, ruled his conduct negligent and suspended him from duty for six months; the verdict eventually read in every military post in the Empire. At age 59, in 1822, Procter died at Bath, England. Governor General Sir George Prevost had been ordered to appear before a court martial inquiring into his management of the British war effort, but he died, in 1816, before his peers could investigate him. Sir James Yeo left Canada, more or less unscathed by the events of the conflict, only to die while at sea in 1818.

In 1822, after eight years on the beach, Robert Barclay wrote for assistance from a friend in the government claiming that the parliamentary squabble had done him a disservice.[17] His appeal must have worked, because in April 1824 Barclay was recalled to active duty and placed in charge of a bomb-ketch, a small vessel mounting one or two huge mortars. The "bomb" was named the *Infernal*, and Barclay took it to Algiers, where an international dispute was raging.

Robert Barclay returned to England five months later and was formally commissioned as a post captain. With that preferred rank he returned to Edinburgh and resumed his family life, never to go to sea again. As a captain on half pay, his income supplemented with a pension earned by his numerous war wounds, Barclay could wait for his name to rise up the over-populated seniority list towards the rank of admiral. The Barclay home in Saxe-Cobourg Place became a busy household blessed with the birth of eight children, two of whom married (one of them to a naval officer) and produced grandchildren. On May 8, 1837, in his fifty-second year, the one-armed Royal Navy veteran, still a captain, died and was buried in the historic Greyfriars churchyard. A single sentence was inscribed to remember him, carved as a footnote on a monument Barclay himself had erected over two of his children who had died in infancy.

Unlike the men who sailed them, some of the warships of Lake Erie returned from their graves to assume a second incarnation.[18] The *Lawrence, Detroit* and *Queen Charlotte* had

126

Almost a year after the battle, August 12, 1814, the British captured the *Somers* and the *Ohio* in a daring cutting-out expedition off Fort Erie.

remained at Put-in-Bay throughout the winter of 1813/14. Stephen Champlin had been sent there in December to arm them in the event that a British attempt to reclaim them should be mounted. A scheme to cross the ice of Lake Erie with a company of men and recapture the vessels was discussed by Yeo and Prevost, but nothing ever came of the plan. In the spring the *Detroit* and *Queen Charlotte* were brought down to Presque Isle. The *Lawrence*, *Niagara* and remaining ships in the American squadron joined them the next year, after seeing some limited action. The events of 1814 had reduced the strength of the American squadron. The *Trippe*, *Little Belt*, *Ariel* and *Chippawa* were destroyed in December 1813, during a British raid upon Black Rock and Buffalo. The following summer the *Scorpion* and *Tigress* were taken by a small group of Royal Navy men and Indians on Lake Huron, and the *Somers* and *Ohio* were captured off Fort Erie. With the declaration of peace, the *Caledonia*, *General Hunter*, *Lady Prevost* and *Porcupine* were sold into the merchant service, with the latter schooner surviving into the 1850s.

The larger warships were mothballed in the style of the early nineteenth century. The *Lawrence*, *Detroit* and *Queen Charlotte*, their masts removed, were moored in Misery Bay, a circular cove near the mouth of the Presque Isle harbour, and then scuttled. The *Niagara* was used as a receiving ship until 1818, when it too was stripped down and sunk beside the others. Although a peace treaty had ended the fighting and things appeared to be getting back to normal, there was still a fear that war would erupt again. It made sense for the Americans to keep the once-proud warships safe from the ravages of the weather, so a renewed call to arms could be answered with readily available cruisers.

Peace prospered, however, and the ships remained beneath the waters. All four were eventually sold in 1825 to a Commander Budd, who resold them on August 9 of that year to a Mr. Benjamin Brown for a measly $325. After ten years and two more sales, they came into the possession of Captain George Miles. In 1837 the *Detroit* and *Queen Charlotte* were raised and refitted for merchant duty.

The *Lawrence* and *Niagara* remained sunken for many more years. In 1860, in preparation for the dedication of the Perry monument at Cleveland, wood was retrieved from the

127

Lawrence and fashioned into several armchairs, two of which were presented to Usher Parsons and Stephen Champlin both of whom were then in their seventies. In 1875 a plan was concocted to raise Perry's original flagship for display at Philadelphia, during the American centennial celebrations the following year. Only the keel and rotted timbers remained of the once proud ship. Nevertheless, it was transported to Philadelphia, where it proved to be a poor draw and ended up on the block at a sheriff's auction.

A more glorious end was awaiting the *Niagara*. As the centenary celebrations of the battle were being formulated, a scheme was developed to raise the *Niagara* and restore it to its former condition. This feat was accomplished in time for a fitting replica of the warship, built on the bones of the original vessel, to be towed by the steamship *Wolverine* on a tour around the Great Lakes and back to Put-in-Bay on September 10, 1913 for the

Stephen Champlin lived to become a commodore, survive the Civil War and see the birth of the country called Canada.

dedication of the Perry Memorial, a 110-metre granite column that had been erected there. Moored at Erie, the *Niagara* was later allowed to fall into disrepair until it was taken over by the Pennsylvania government. After more than seventy years of partial restorations, the brig was completely rebuilt in 1988 and relaunched on the 175th anniversary of the battle.

The *Queen Charlotte* and *Detroit* did not last long as merchantmen, but the days of the former British flagship were not allowed to end until it had been involved in a most bizarre twist of coincidence. The old corvette was discovered in 1841 a derelict, dismantled at Buffalo and purchased by a group of merchants from Niagara Falls, New York. This group of entrepreneurs wanted to make some money by using the vessel as a spectacle that would go careening over Niagara Falls. They also had in mind the possibility of making a political statement.

The *Detroit* was dragged down the Niagara River and moored at Grand Island. Then, someone with a paint brush added a new name on its side and therein made the link with the more glorious past of Barclay's flagship. In 1840 William Henry Harrison (the same Harrison who had joined Oliver Hazard Perry to defeat Henry Procter) made his second bid for the office of president of the United States. He ran beneath the slogan "Tippecanoe and Tyler too," coined to capitalize on his 1811 attack on an Indian village and the name of his running mate, John Tyler. Harrison won the election, but on his inaugural day he presented a lengthy speech out-of-doors and caught a fatal bout of pneumonia. His vice-president became the first to take office from a fallen leader and, subsequently, also became the first president to be threatened with impeachment. Tyler had the habit of vetoing legislation of which he disapproved. One set of bills dealt with the banking system and his repeated vetoes aroused the ire of many citizens. A group of these citizens lived in the Niagara Falls area. As a result, an eyewitness to the last voyage of Barclay's flagship noted:

> With the aid of a spy-glass we could perceive, that she had been rechristened *Veto*, which name was painted on her in large letters—a hint to the President, that he had better 'mind his eye' or his opposition . . . may cause him a journey similar to that which the Buffalo people have given to his veto."[19]

William Henry Harrison (1773-1841) joined the U.S. Army in 1791 and lived to serve briefly as his country's ninth president.

At 3:00 pm on Wednesday, September 15, 1841, (the tenth had been considered for the spectacle, but was rejected as being disrespectful to the memory of Perry's victory) two boatloads of men hauled the *Detroit* out into the current of the upper Niagara River for her final voyage. The line was cast off, and the ship headed downriver. Opposite to popular belief, it went without any cargo. One story claims that animals had been tied on board as some kind of cruel exhibition, as had been done on the *Michigan* in 1827. Eyewitness accounts do not support this version of the events. Instead, the aged warship, the last of its kind to be constructed at the Amherstburg Naval Establishment, went alone to its fate.

She took the first plunge gallantly head on, and for a moment seemed completely engulfed, but almost instantly the hull shot upwards from "the hell of waters," her main and foremasts went by the board, and on she went. The next descent was passed safely. At the third, the mizen mast gave away, and a few rods farther she grounded by the head. Her stern swung slowly round and grounded also. When we left Goat Island, she was lying broadside to the current, in its shallowest part, nearly midway between the island and the Canadian shore.[20]

In the following months HMS *Detroit* broke up in the rapids. It disappeared, forgotten, in the waters that flow from Lake Erie to the sea.

CHAPTER NOTES

Chapter notes have been prepared to provide references for direct quotations, for certain significant points and for background information that does not fit smoothly into the text. The notes feature abbreviated authors' names and titles, which are given in full in the bibliography.

Modern spellings of place names have been used in the text. The spelling and grammatical constructions of direct quotations have been preserved (with a very few exceptions) in order to convey a sense of the personalities behind the pens.

CHAPTER ONE: The War Along The Lakes

1. A. T. Mahan, *Sea Power . . . War of 1812.* Vol. 1, pp. 301-302.

2. Chauncey to Hamilton, September 26, 1812, William S. Dudley, *Naval War of 1812: A Documentary History*, Vol. 1, pp. 314-315 (Hereafter: *Dudley*).

3. Hamilton to Dobbins, September 15, 1812, *Ibid*, p. 310.

4. Elliott to Chauncey, October 9, 1812, *Ibid*, pp. 328-331.

5. William Wood, *Select British Documents of the Canadian War of 1812*, Vol. 1, pp. 246-247 (Hereafter: Wood). For a detailed study of the Provincial Marine, see the paper by W. A. B. Douglas, entitled "The Anatomy of Naval Incompetence . . . ."

6. Gray to Prevost, March 12, 1813, Cruikshank, *The Documentary History . . . 1812-1814*, Vol. 5, pp. 107-109 (Hereafter: *Cruikshank*).

7. Gray to Prevost, December 3, 1812, National Archives of Canada (NAC), RG8 series, Vol. 728, (Microfilm Reel # C-3243), pp. 135-136.

8. Chauncey to Hamilton, December 9, 1812, *Dudley*, pp. 365, 367.

9. Prevost to Bathurst, October 17, 1812, NAC, Q Series, Vol. 118, (Microfilm Reel # C-11919), p. 275.

CHAPTER TWO: Robert Barclay, R. N.

1. Two main sources form the basis of the biographical information about Robert Barclay. They are: Blanche Burt's "Captain Robert Heriott Barclay, R. N." and John Marshall's "Captains of 1824" in Marshall's *Naval Biography*, Volume 3, Part I.

2. David White, *The Frigate Diana*, pp. 13-14.

3.   Barclay Court Martial Narrative, *Wood*, Vol. 2, p. 298. Admiral Borlase's letter to the Admiralty announcing the officers being sent to the lakes was dated March 10, 1813 at Bermuda. This, and the enclosed list of officers, may be found on NAC, MG 12 Microfilm #B-1448 Admiralty, Secretary's Dept. In-Letters Admiral Despatches North America 1812–1813 Admiralty 1, vol. 503, pp. 178-179.

4.   Prevost to Bathurst, April 21, 1813, *Cruikshank*, Vol. 5, p. 158.

5.   General Order, Quebec, April 22, 1813, *Wood*, Vol. 2, pp. 81-84.

6.   Barclay to Freer, May 9, 1813, *Ibid*, Vol. 1, pp. 115-119.

7.   *Ibid.*

8.   *Ibid.*

9.   *Ibid.*

10.   *Ibid.*

11.   Cited in "The Sailor Who Lost," *The Windsor Evening Record*, October 6, 1877.

CHAPTER THREE: From Kingston to Lake Erie

1.   Biographical information regarding Sir James Lucas Yeo comes mainly from John W. Spurr's paper, "Sir James Lucas Yeo, A Hero on the Lakes."

2.   Barclay Court Martial Narrative, *Wood*, Vol. 2, p. 298.

3.   Barclay to Yeo, June 1, 1813, NAC MG 12, Adm. 1, Vol. 5445 (Admiralty and Secretariat Papers: In-Letters Reports of Courts Martial, 1814, September), (Microfilm Reel # C-12856), p. 71. The series of unpublished letters contained in this volume are hereafter referred to as *The Barclay Letters*.

4.   Prevost to Bathurst, June 1, 1813, *Wood*, Vol. 2, p. 31.

5.   David Wingfield, "Four Years on the Lakes of Canada . . .," NAC MG 24 F-18, p. 10.

6.   Barclay to Yeo, June 1, 1813, *The Barclay Letters*, p. 74.

7.   *Ibid*, p. 72.

8.   *Ibid*, pp. 73-74.

9.   A more complete review of the history of the area along the Detroit River may be found in David Botsford's "History of Bois Blanc Island" and *At the End of the Trail* and E. J. LaJeunesse's "First Four Years of the Settlement . . . ."

10.   Barclay to Yeo, June 7, 1813, *The Barclay Letters*, p. 79.

11.   Biographical information regarding Major General Henry Procter is sparse. See the *MacMillan Dictionary of Canadian Biography* and Ermatinger's "Retreat of Procter and Tecumseh." According to Irving's *Officers of the British Forces in Canada during the War*

of 1812-15, pp. 9, 11, Procter's promotion record was as follows: Captain of the 43d Regiment 30 Nov. 1792; Major 1795; Lt. Colonel of the 41st Regiment 9 Oct. 1800; Brigadier General (local) 8 Feb. 1813; Major General 4 June 1813.

12.   Procter to Prevost, July 4, 1813, *Wood*, Vol. 2, p. 9.

13.   Barclay to Yeo, June 7, 1813, *The Barclay Letters*, p. 78.

14.   Barclay to Yeo, June 16, 1813, *The Barclay Letters*, p. 82.

15.   *Ibid*, pp. 82-83.

16.   Barclay to Vincent, June 17, 1813, *Wood*, Vol. 2, pp. 245-247. Barclay to Harvey, June (unnumbered, probably 19 or 20, 1813), *The Barclay Letters*, pp. 84-86. When Barclay and Vincent met for the first time in late May, Vincent was a Brigadier General. According to Irving's *Officers of the British Forces*, he was promoted to Major General on June 4, 1813, at the same time as Henry Procter was promoted.

17.   Dobbins and Dobbins, "The Dobbins Papers," p. 322 (Hereafter: *Dobbins Papers*).

CHAPTER FOUR: Oliver Hazard Perry, U. S. N.

1.   Biographical information regarding Oliver Hazard Perry may be found in James Barnes' *The Hero of Erie*, pp. 139-142 of Barnes' *Naval Actions of the War of 1812* and Richard Dillon's *We Have Met the Enemy*. . . .

2.   Perry to Hamilton, two letters, November 10, 1812, *Dudley*, Vol. 1, pp. 564-565.

3.   Parsons, *Battle of Lake Erie*, pp. 33-34 (Hereafter: *Parsons*).

4.   Perry to Hamilton, November 28, 1812, *Dudley*, p. 354.

5.   Since one metre is equal to about 39 inches in the English Standard system of measurement, the 15.5 m. by 5.1 m. dimensions of the smaller gunboats would have been equal to 50 feet by 17 feet.

6.   For a detailed account of the building of the Lake Erie squadron, see Max Rosenburg's *The Building of Perry's Fleet* . . ., which may be supplemented by Stacey's "Another Look at the Battle of Lake Erie."

7.   Re: Brown's comment about the slowness of the supply line, see Rosenburg, p. 15.

8.   *Dobbins Papers*, p. 317.

9.   Parsons, *Battle of Lake Erie*, p. 5.

10.   Benson J. Lossing, *The Pictorial Field-Book of the War of 1812*, p. 512.

11.   Perry to Jones, June 20, 1813, *Cruikshank*, Vol. 8, p. 3.

12.   Conversion of metric dimensions for Perry's brigs yields these dimensions of length, breadth and draught: *Lawrence* and *Niagara* 34 m. by 9 m. by 2.8 m.=110 ft. by 30 ft. by 9 ft.

13.   *Dobbins Papers*, p. 324.

CHAPTER FIVE: Problems at Amherstburg

1.   Since few precise measurements of the British Lake Erie squadron appear to have survived, the exact size of each ship must be based upon various perceptions of the ships and upon comparison to their contemporaries on Lake Ontario from which measurements were taken by the Admiralty in 1815.

        Conversion of the metric dimensions of the larger vessels in the Lake Erie Provincial Marine yield these approximate dimensions of length, beam and draught:

        Queen Charlotte – 31 m. by 8 m. by 3.5 m. = 101 ft. by 27.6 ft. by 12 ft. (based on dimensions of *Royal George*, see footnote 9 below);

        Lady Prevost – 22 m. by 6.4 m. by less than 3 m. = 71 ft. by 21 ft. by less than 9 ft. (based on dimensions of the schooner *Prince Regent* ordered at same time as *Lady Prevost* and launched at York in July 1812, given in Stacey's *Ship's of the British Squadron*, p. 219.);

        General Hunter – 26 m. by 5.4 m. by 2.4 m. = 84 ft. by 18 ft. by 8 ft. (based on Admiralty drawing in Douglas's "The Anatomy of Naval Incompetence," p. 7).

    Estimations of burthen vary considerably among the many sources. Roosevelt, in *The Naval War of 1812*, set large amounts, giving the *Queen Charlotte*, for instance, a burthen of 400 tonnes. Contemporary estimates were considerably less than that. A report on the Provincial Marine in August of 1811 placed the corvette's burthen at 180 tonnes (see *Wood*, Vol. 1, pp. 246-247). As described in Robert Dodge's text, any one of four different formulas could be used to determine the tonnage of cargo a ship could potentially carry. The figures used in this text follow those attributed to Daniel Dobbins, since they provide a consistent standard for all the ships from both squadrons and are more in line with estimates given by people familiar with the ships.

2.   The exact arrangement of ordnance upon each of the British ships, prior to the battle, is difficult to confirm. There appears to have been a variety of arrangements in the months leading up to the battle. The *Queen Charlotte*, for instance, is reported to have had the following batteries:

        September 16, 1811 – fourteen 12-pounder carronades (although sixteen 24-pounder carronades appear to have been ordered) (*Wood*, Vol. 1, p. 239-240);

        February 24, 1812 – ten 24-pounder carronades and six long guns (*Wood*, Vol. 1, p.254);

        March 13, 1813 – twelve 24-pounder carronades and four long 9-pounders (*Cruikshank*, Vol. 5, p. 109);

        July 24, 1813 – eighteen 24-pounder carronades (*Cruikshank*, Vol. 6, p. 270).

    This final description was given by Robert Barclay and was used as the basis for representing the ordnance of his squadron during the early part of the summer of 1813.

3.   Barclay to Yeo, June 7, 1813, *The Barclay Letters*, p. 73.

4.   Barclay to Yeo, June 1, *Ibid*, p. 73.

5.   Report re: Provincial Marine by A. H. Pye, December 7, 1811, *Wood*, Vol. 1. p. 241.

6.   *Ibid.*

7.   Barclay to Yeo, June 7, 1813, *The Barclay Letters*, p. 78.

8.   Gray to Prevost, December 11, 1812, NAC RG 8C series, (Microfilm Reel # C-3243), Vol. 728, p. 122.

9.   Since William Bell's measurements of the *Detroit* have not surfaced, assumptions must be made about the size of the *Detroit*. It was based on the *Royal George* class and so was at least the size of the *Queen Charlotte*. All sources identify the *Detroit* as being the largest of the ships involved in the battle, however. The dimensions used in this text are based on the specifications by which the directors of Project HMS Detroit in Amherstburg, Ontario, plan to build their replica of Barclay's flagship: 34 m. by 8.6 m. by 3.6 m. or 110 ft. by 28.5 ft. by 12 ft.

10.   NAC RG 8C series, Vol. 729, (Microfilm Reel # C-3243), pp. 74-76.

11.   Re: iron making in Upper Canada—English iron master John Mason built an iron works near Long Point in 1817, the first in Upper Canada. It collapsed, literally, the next year. Henry Barrett, *Lore and Legends of Long Point*, p. 80.

12.   NAC RG 8C series, Vol. 729, (Microfilm Reel # C-3243), p. 3.

13.   Barclay to Yeo, June 7, 1813, *The Barclay Letters*, pp. 78-79.

14.   Barclay to Procter, June 29, 1813, *Wood*, Vol 2, p. 249.

15.   *Ibid.*

16.   Barclay to Yeo, June 7, 1813, *The Barclay Letters*, p. 74.

17.   Barclay to Procter, June 7, 1813, *The Barclay Letters*, p. 80 and Barclay to Procter, June 9, 1813, *Ibid*, p. 81.

18.   Procter to Sheaffe, January 13, 1813, *Wood*, Vol. 2, p. 3.

19.   Yeo to Barclay, May 20, 1814 (This date appears to be a copying error, since Barclay's orders were issued during May of 1813), *The Barclay Letters*, pp. 41-44.

20.   See Irving's *Officers of the British Forces*, pp. 204-207 for brief biographies about Irvine and Rolette.

21.   Gray to Prevost, March 12, 1813, *Cruikshank*, Vol. 5, p. 107.

22.   Barclay to Yeo, July 19, 1813, *The Barclay Letters*, p. 92.

23.   Barclay to Hall, August 14, *Wood*, Vol. 2, pp. 259-260.

24.   Hall to Barclay, August 14, *Ibid.*

25.   Barclay to Gilmor, August 14, 1813, *The Barclay Letters*, p. 100.

26.   Hall to Freer, August 15, 1813, NAC RG 8C series Vol. 730, (Microfilm Reel # C-3243), p. 93.

27.   Freer to Procter, August 25, 1813, *Cruikshank*, Vol. 7, p. 62.

CHAPTER NOTES

CHAPTER SIX: The Failed Blockade

1.   Barclay to Yeo, June 7, 1813, *The Barclay Letters*, p. 78.

2.   Barclay to Vincent, June 17, 1813, *Wood*, Vol. 2, p. 246.

3.   *Ibid* and Barclay to Harvey, June (unnumbered, probably 19 or 20, 1813). *The Barclay Letters*, pp. 84-86.

4.   Barclay to Yeo, June 16, 1813, *The Barclay Letters*, p. 82.

5.   Vincent to Prevost, June 18, 1813, *Wood*, Vol. 2, p. 245.

6.   Prevost to Procter, June 20, 1813, *Cruikshank*, Vol. 6, p. 101.

7.   Procter to Prevost, July 11, 1813, *Wood*, Vol. 2, p. 253.

8.   De Rottenburg to Procter, July 1, 1813, *Cruikshank*, Vol.6, pp. 171-172.

9.   Barclay Court Martial Narrative, *Wood*, Vol. 2, p. 301.

10.   Barclay to Prevost, July 16, 1813, *Ibid*, p. 259.

11.   Barclay to Yeo, July 19, 1813, *The Barclay Letters*, p. 89.

12.   "National Intelligencer," August 7, 1813, *Cruikshank*, Vol.6, pp. 267-268.

13.   Perry to Jones, July 19, 1813, *Ibid*, Vol. 8, p. 5.

14.   "National Intelligencer," *Cruikshank*, Vol.6, pp. 267-268.

15.   Barclay to Yeo, July 19, 1813, *The Barclay Letters*, p. 90.

16.   Perry to Jones, July 23, 1813, *Cruikshank*, Vol. 8, p. 6.

17.   Holmes to Perry, July 23, 1813, *Ibid*, p. 7.

18.   Perry to Jones, July 27, 1813, *Ibid*, p. 6.

19.   *Dobbins Papers*, p. 330.

20.   *Ibid.*, p. 331.

21.   As with the British squadron, there are discrepancies in the various sources regarding the ordnance carried aboard the American ships. The data shown here is taken from Dodge's "The Battle of Lake Erie," p. 15. It agrees with the amounts shown by Roosevelt, p. 242, and Drake's paper on "Artillery and Its Influences . . .," except in slight differences accredited to the smaller vessels. Dobbins, on p. 336, presents an appreciably different list of guns, although all sources agree on the armament of the brigs.

22.   *Dobbins Papers*, p. 335.

CHAPTER SEVEN: The Complaints of August

1.   Barclay Court Martial Narrative, *Wood*, Vol. 2, p. 302.

2.   *Ibid.*

3. Barclay to Stuart, July 29, 1813, *The Barclay Letters*, p. 94.

4. Memoir of Amelia Harris, in J. James *Loyalist Narratives from Upper Canada*, p. 145.

5. *Ibid*. It is not likely that Barclay gave passage from Amherstburg to an officer's widow aboard the *Queen Charlotte*, since he had been away from Amherstburg for more than two weeks. The *Chippawa* had been noted as missing from the squadron by the Americans. During those two weeks Barclay also received news of Procter's venture to Fort Meigs. Perhaps the news and the widow arrived aboard the *Chippawa* or the transport *Mary*. A key word here is *perhaps*, since many of the events of this period are cloaked in uncertainty.

6. *Dobbins Papers*, p. 333.

7. Barclay's message was contained in two despatches: Colonel F. Battersby to Colonel Edward Baynes, July 31, 1813, *Cruikshank*, Vol. 6, pp. 295-296, and De Rottenburg to Freer, August 1, 1813, *Ibid*, p. 297.

8. Barclay to Yeo, July 19, 1813, *The Barclay Letters*, p. 90.

9. Barclay to Hall, July 21, 1813, *Ibid*, pp. 93-94.

10. Barclay to Yeo, August 5, 1813, *Ibid*, p. 98.

11. James, *Loyalist Narratives*, p. 147.

12. Gilmor to Couche, August 6, 1813, *Cruikshank*, Vol. 6, p. 317.

13. Prevost to Procter, August. 22, 1813, *Wood*, Vol. 2, pp. 48-49.

14. Regarding the crews in Yeo's squadron, July 24, 1813, *Cruikshank*, Vol. 6 , p. 269.

15. Chauncey to Perry, July 13, 1813, *Ibid*, Vol. 8, pp. 9-10.

16. Perry to Jones, August 10, 1813, *Ibid*, pp. 8-9.

17. Jones to Perry, August 18, 1813, *Ibid*, p. 11.

18. *Parsons*, p. 7.

19. *Ibid*, p. 8.

20. *Dobbins Papers*, p. 338.

21. Gilmor to Procter, August 14, 1813, *Cruikshank*, Vol. 7, pp. 20-21.

22. Procter to Prevost, August 29, 1813, *Wood*, Vol. 2, pp. 266-267.

23. The "anonymous correspondent" reference appeared in a letter sent by Prevost to Procter on September 6, 1813 (*Wood*, Vol. 2, pp. 270-271.) It was the third in an exchange of comments regarding a rumour that had reached Prevost's ears about dissension between the services at Amherstburg. Procter, in his letter of August 29, indignantly denied the suggestion and expressed his hope that Prevost would allow him "to meet the Insidious." On September 6 Prevost assured Procter that his confidence was restored and that when

time permitted they would "ferret out the Villain." This episode presents another example of the conflicts among individuals that may have influenced the defense of the Right Division.

CHAPTER EIGHT: War Councils

1. Captain Peter Chambers to Freer, August 22, 1813, *Cruikshank*, Vol. 7, p. 48.

2. *Dobbins Papers*, p. 340.

3. Elliott to General Peter Porter, September 1, 1813, *Cruikshank*, pp. 94-95.

4. Barclay to Yeo, September 1, 1813, *Wood*, Vol. 2. pp. 267-269.

5. Although the British squadron suffered from a lack of suitable ordnance, there has been no shortage in the amount of debate regarding the precise strength of that ordnance. The figures presented in this text agree with the testimony of Francis Purvis at the Barclay Court Martial (*Wood*, Vol. 2, p. 315), with the exception of three guns being accorded to the *Little Belt* as *all* other sources attest. For various descriptions and discussions of the British firepower see Roosevelt, Dodge and Drake.

6. Barclay to Yeo, August 17, 1813, *The Barclay Letters*, p. 103.

7. Mahan, *Sea Power and Its Relations to the War of 1812*, p. 77.

8. Barclay to Procter, August 22, 1813, *The Barclay Letters*, p. 105.

9. Barclay Court Martial Narrative, *Wood*, Vol. 2, p. 317.

10. Barclay to Procter, August 14, 1813, *The Barclay Letters*, p. 100.

11. Barclay asked for the red cloth in a letter to Procter on August 16, 1813, *Ibid*, p. 101. His requests for money to pay his men were in letters to Procter, August 16, 1813, *Ibid*, p. 101, to Yeo on August 17, 1813, *Ibid*, pp. 102-103 and to O'Connor on August 18, 1813, *Ibid*, pp. 103, 104.

12. Barclay to Yeo, September 1, *Wood*, Vol. 2, p. 268.

13. *Dobbins Papers*, pp. 340-341.

14. *Ibid.*

15. Gilmor to Couche, September 5, 1813, *Wood*, Vol. 2, pp. 291-292.

16. Procter to Prevost, September 6, 1813, *Ibid*, pp. 269-270.

17. Barclay to Yeo, September 6, 1813, *Ibid*, pp. 292-293. Barclay's note that "I know something of the few that have arrived . . ." may indicate that his reinforcements were not of high quality. Lieutenant George Inglis had been found to be drunk and disobedient on one occasion by Commodore Yeo, an event that lead to Yeo's call for a court martial for Inglis in 1815. (See a series of letters from Yeo to the Admiralty in NAC MG 12 Microfilm #2942 Admiralty and Secretary's Letters In-Letters Captains' Letters "Y" Admiralty 1, vol. 2738, pp. 155-200.)

CHAPTER NINE: The Battle

1. *Dobbins Papers*, p. 345.

2. The final ration of spirits (rum, wine or whatever else was available) had been saved by the British for the day of battle. The crews had gone without their daily toddy for some time before September 10, according to Thomas Stokoe at Barclay's Court Martial, *Wood*, Vol. 2, p. 312.

3. Elliott Court of Inquiry, *Inland Seas*, Vol. 40, p. 114.

4. Barclay to Yeo, September 12, 1813, *Wood*, Vol. 2, p. 275.

5. Barclay Court Martial Narrative, *Wood*, Vol. 2, p. 13.

6. Lieutenant John Yarnell reported conditions aboard the flagship and the distance between the *Lawrence* and the British line as 228.6 metres (250 yards) and the distance between the *Lawrence* and the *Niagara* during the early phase of the battle as one kilometre (3/4 mile) at the Elliott Court of Inquiry, *Inland Seas*, Vol. 40, p. 114.

7. Casselman, *Richardson's War of 1812*, p. 194.

8. Barclay to Yeo, September 12, 1813, *Wood*, Vol. 2, p. 275.

9. *Parsons*, p. 13.

10. *Ibid.* Parsons reported the midshipman's name as being Henry Lamb. The young officer's name actually was Henry Laub (see Emerson's "The Perry's Victory Centenary," p. 247.) To avoid confusion, the quotation from Parson's memorial used here has been altered to show the name "Laub."

11. No casualties were reported to have been suffered on the *Little Belt*, which was larger and more heavily armed than the *Chippawa*, and no mention was made of the sloop or its commander in Barclay's account. These circumstances suggest that the *Little Belt* was handled poorly during the battle, avoiding involvement in the heat of action when even its meagre battery could have been used to support the *Detroit* and *Queen Charlotte*.

12. Taylor, "Battle of Lake Erie," p. 157.

13. Barclay to Yeo, September 12, 1813, *Wood*, Vol.2 p. 275.

14. *Ibid.*

15. *Parsons*, p. 10.

16. Elliott Court Martial, *Wood*, p. 114.

17. *Ibid*, p. 117.

18. Elliott, "Speech . . .," p. 9.

19. Clinton, "Life of Stephen Champlin," p. 392.

20. *Ibid.*

CHAPTER NOTES

21.   Inglis to Barclay, September 10, 1813, *Wood*, Vol. 2, p. 278.

22.   Elliott, *Wood*, Vol. 2, p. 8.

23.   *Parsons*, p. 14.

24.   George Bancroft, *Oliver Hazard Perry. . .*, p. 27.

CHAPTER TEN: "This Victory, So Decisive and Important"

1.   *The Perry's Victory Centenary Report*, p. 153.

2.   Barnes, *Naval Actions of the War of 1812*, p. 88.

3.   Bancroft, *Oliver Hazard Perry . . .*, p. 29.

4.   Casselman, *Richardson's War of 1812*, pp. 200-203.

5.   Barclay to Yeo, September 12, 1813, *Wood*, Vol. 2, pp. 274-277.

6.   In an appendix to Casselman's *War of 1812*, p. 305, there is a copy of a letter from a Colonel Brush to Colonel Askin dated October 20, 1813 mentioning that Dr. Richardson would be allowed to return home as soon as he felt that Barclay could be left in American hands. Surgeon George Young who travelled to Amherstburg with Barclay and later appeared at his court martial is not listed as wounded (see *Wood*, Vol. 2, pp. 279-281) nor as a prisoner of war (on a list obtained at the library of the Fort Malden National Park). Perhaps he and Richardson worked as a team to save the gravely injured commander. It is assumed that Young stayed with Barclay during his recovery and return to England.

7.   Prisoners of war received the same kind of treatment in 1813 as they have in recent times. During the year of captivity the men from Barclay's squadron were joined by other British prisoners, some from the defeat at Moraviantown. Throughout the time, they were visited by government representatives who encouraged them to defect. The officers were kept separate from the rank and file. In July 1814 an exchange was organized and most of the men were marched back to Sandusky arriving there on August 18. It was not until October 25 that three shiploads of prisoners arrived at Long Point. The condition of the men was very poor, owing to the many privations they had suffered. In prison and on the march many had been left without boots and given no medical attention. Dysentry and fevers incapacitated most of the men. Tents were not provided for their encampments and "the men complained that they were half-starved . . . what they got was not fit to be eaten, as it smelt and was unwholesome." (Cruikshank's article about the Royal Newfoundland Regiment, p.15.) Of those who arrived at Long Point on the twenty-fifth, it was predicted that not one in twenty would regain his former health. For detailed accounts of the prisoners see Cruikshank's "The Royal Newfoundland Regiment" and Casselman's biography of Richardson.

8.   Procter to De Rottenburg, September 12, 1813, *Wood*, Vol. 2, pp. 272-273.

9.   Cited in Casselman, *Richardson's War of 1812*, p. 205.

10.   *Dobbins Papers*, p. 361.

11. Yeo to Warren, October 10, 1813, *Cruikshank*, Vol. 7, pp. 219-220.

12. Prevost's General Order, November 24, 1813, *Wood*, Vol. 2, pp. 294-297.

13. Yeo to Warren, November 14, *Cruikshank*, Vol. 8, p. 180.

14. Samuel Hambleton, purser aboard the *Lawrence*, had served with Perry at Newport and requested active duty during the battle in which he was wounded. Hambleton was made prize master by the Navy Department after the battle and was responsible for organizing the financial rewards for the victory. This was done according to the value of the captured ships and a formula that divided that amount among the participants and Commander in Chief Chauncey. One person who was excluded from the list was Daniel Dobbins, since he had been absent during the fight. Dobbins appealed and received $2,295 late in 1815. Of the more than $250,000 awarded, $3,066 remained unclaimed as of 1847. For the details of prize money see Howell's paper on Purser Hambleton.

15. Cited in Lossing, *Pictorial Field-book . . .*, p. 535.

16. Chauncey to Perry, October 9, 1813, *Cruikshank*, Vol. 7, pp. 43-45.

17. *The Times of London*, Monday, November 8, 1813, p. 3.

18. *Ibid*, Friday, November 12, 1813, p. 3.

CHAPTER ELEVEN: Men and Ships

1. Casselman, *Richardson's War of 1812*, p. 244.

2. Chauncey to Jones, October 13, 1813, *Cruikshank*, Vol. 8, pp. 55-56.

3. Charles Askin, a militiaman working with the commissariat of the force on the Niagara Peninsula, dined with Barclay at Dickson's in Queenston in December. (See *Cruikshank*, Vol. 9. pp. 26-28.) Another witness to Barclay at Queenston was Ebernezer Howe who frequently saw the commander walking in the town (See Howe's "Recollections . . .").

4. Memo for Prevost by Barclay, April 12, 1814, *Cruikshank*, pp. 288-289.

5. Procter to Barclay, June 5, 1814, *The Barclay Letters*, p. 62 and Gilmor to Barclay, June 9 (?), 1814, *Ibid*, pp. 63-64.

6. Burt, "Captain Robert H. Barclay . . .," p. 177.

7. "Lake Erie Court Martial Papers" in *Wood*, Vol. 2, pp. 289-319.

8. *Ibid*, p. 318.

9. For the details of the parliamentary comments regarding the battle and their possible effect on Barclay's career, see Peckham's paper "Commodore Perry's Captive."

10. Barclay to Yeo, September 12, 1813, *Wood*, Vol. 2, p. 275.

11. Taylor to his brother, October 17, 1813, cited in *The Perry's Victory Centenary*, p. 158.

12.   Elliott to Perry, September 17, 1813, *Cruikshank*, Vol. 7, p. 148.

13.   Perry to Elliott, September 18, 1813, *Ibid.*

14.   *Parsons*, p. 19.

15.   "Testimony in the Court of Enquiry on Captain Elliott . . .," *Inland Seas*. Vol. 40, pp. 110-119, 131.

16.   The interpersonal problems in Jesse Elliott's career did not end with the War of 1812. Starting in 1833 he became involved with the USS *Constitution*, later using it as his flagship when he was commodore of the Mediterranean squadron. During that time he collected rare artifacts and livestock for friends and colleagues back home, turning the proud frigate into "Elliott's Ark." That act of impropriety combined with complaints regarding his performance as commander led to his suspension. Four years later a change in the Washington administration caused him to be reinstated. He served as commandant of the Philadelphia Navy Yard until his death. For the details in Elliott's handling of the *Constitution* see Martin's, *A Most Fortunate Ship*, pp. 195-213. For recent treatments of the Perry-Elliott controversy, see the articles written by Belovarac and by Runyan and Copes.

17.   Peckham, "Perry's Captive."

18.   For a description of the fates of the vessels that took part in the battle, see Severance's "What Became of Perry's Fleet." Other resources include Bauer's "List of United States Warships" and Macpherson's "List of Vessels . . . on the Great Lakes, 1755-1875." The story of the *Scorpion* and *Tigress* and their debatable discovery may be found in Elsie M. Jury's papers published in 1959 and 1972. A discussion of the restoration efforts and most recent launch of the brig *Niagara* may be found in "The Ship That Didn't Give Up" by Malcomson and Malcomson. A similar article is Carone's "Preserving the U.S. Brig *Niagara*," although Carone presents evidence that the brig preserved at Erie may indeed be the *Lawrence* rather than the *Niagara*.

19.   Report from the *Niagara Chronicle*, cited in *The St. Catharines Journal*, Thursday, October 7, 1841.

20.   Report from the *Buffalo Common Advocate*, cited in *The St.Catharines Journal*, Thursday, October 7, 1841.

BIBLIOGRAPHY

Bancroft, George. *Oliver Hazard Perry and The Battle of Lake Erie.* Rhode Island: Department of Education, 1913.

Barnes, James. *The Hero of Lake Erie (Oliver Hazard Perry).* New York: D. Appleton and Company, 1898.

Barnes, James. *Naval Actions of the War of 1812.* New York: Harper and Brothers Publisher, 1896.

Barrett, Harry B. *Lore and Legends of Long Point.* Don Mills: Burns and MacEachern, 1977.

Bauer, K. J. "List of United States Warships on the Great Lakes 1796-1941." *Ontario History.* 56(1964): 58-64.

Belovarac, Allan. "A Brief Overview of the Battle of Lake Erie and the Perry-Elliott Controversy." *The Journal of Erie Studies.* 17(1988):3-6.

Berton, Pierre. *The Invasion of Canada.* Toronto: McClelland and Stewart, 1980.

Berton, Pierre. *Flames Across The Border.* Toronto: McClelland and Stewart, 1981.

Botsford, David P. "The History of Bois Blanc Island." *Ontario History.* 47(1955):132-139.

Botsford, David P. *At the End of the Trail: A Collection of Anecdotal Histories. . . .* Eleanor Gignac, Linda Beare and Effie Botsford, eds. Windsor: Windsor Press and Litho Ltd., 1985.

Buckie, Robert " 'His Majesty's Flag Has Not Been Tarnished': The Role of Robert Heriot Barclay." *The Journal of Erie Studies.* 17(1988):85-102.

Burt, Blanche. "Captain Robert Heriott Barclay, R. N." *Ontario Historical Society Papers and Records.* 14(1916):169-178.

Calvert, George H. *The Battle of Lake Erie.* Providence: Albro, 1854.

Carone, Anthony C. "Preserving the U.S. Brig Niagara, 1913-1988." *The Journal of Erie Studies.* 17(1988):103-112.

Casselman, Alexander, ed. *Richardson's War of 1812.* Toronto: Coles, 1974.

Chapelle, Howard I. *The History of the American Sailing Navy.* New York: Bonanza, 1949.

Clinton, George H. "The Life of Stephen Champlin." *Buffalo Historical Society Publications,* 8(1905):381-400.

BIBLIOGRAPHY

Cooper, James Fenimore. *The Battle of Lake Erie*, Cooperstown: H. E. Phinney, 1843.

Cruikshank, E. A. "Record of the Services of the Canadian Regiments in the War of 1812: Part 1 The Royal Newfoundland Regiment." *Selected Papers from the Transactions of the Canadian Military Institute* no. 5, (1893-1894):5-15.

Cruikshank, E. A., ed. "The Contest For the Command of Lake Erie in 1812-1813." *Royal Society of Canada Transactions*, 6(1899):359-386.

Cruikshank, E. A. *The Documentary History of the Campaign upon the Niagara Frontier 1812-1814.* 9 vols. Welland: Lundy's Lane Historical Society, 1896-1908.

Cruikshank, E. A. "The Contest For the Command of Lake Ontario in 1814." *Ontario Historical Society Papers and Records.* 20(1924):99-159.

Cumberland, Barlow. "The Navies of Lake Ontario in the War of 1812." *Ontario Historical Society Papers and Records.* 8(1907): 124-142.

Dillon, Richard. *We Have Met the Enemy: Oliver Hazard Perry: Wilderness Commodore.* New York: McGraw-Hill, 1978.

Dobbins, Daniel and Dobbins, William. "The Dobbins Papers." *Buffalo Historical Society Publications.* 8,(1905):283-379.

Dodge, Robert J. "The Battle of Lake Erie" A Master of Arts thesis written at Ohio State University in 1961, reprinted May 1986.

Douglas, W. A. B. "The Anatomy of Naval Incompetence: The Provincial Marine in Defence of Upper Canada before 1813." *Ontario History.* 71(1979):3-25.

Drake, Frederick. "A Loss of Mastery: The British Squadron on Lake Erie, May-September 1813." *The Journal of Erie Studies.* 17(1988):47-75.

Drake, Frederick. "Artillery and Its Influence on Naval Tactics: Reflections on the Battle of Lake Erie." Paper presented at the War on the Great Lakes Symposium, University of Windsor, September 10, 1988.

Dudley, William S. *The Naval War of 1812: A Documentary History.* Volume 1. Washington: Historical Center Department of the Navy, 1985.

Elliott, Jesse Duncan. *Speech Delivered in Hagerstown, Md. on 14th November 1843.* Philadelphia: G. B. Zeiber & Co., 1844.

Emerson, George D. *The Perry's Victory Centenary.* Albany: Lyon, 1916.

Ermatinger, Judge. "The Retreat of Procter and Tecumseh." *Ontario Historical Society Papers and Records.* 17(1919):11-21.

Forester, C. S. *The Age of Fighting Sail.* Garden City, New York: Doubleday and Co. Inc., 1956.

Fredriksen, John C. " 'A Grand Moment For Our Beloved Commander': Sailing Master William V. Taylor's Account of the Battle of Lake Erie." *The Journal of Erie Studies.* 17(1988):13-122.

Harris, Amelia. "Historical Memoranda." *Loyalist Narratives from Upper Canada.* Ed. James J. Talman. Toronto: Champlain Society, 1946.

Hitsman, J. Mackay. *The Incredible War of 1812: A Military History.* Toronto: University of Toronto Press, 1972.

Howe, Ebernezer. "Recollections of a Pioneer Printer," *Publication of the Buffalo Historical Society.* 9(1906):377-406.

Howell, William, Maher. "Purser Samuel Hambleton." *Inland Seas.* 36(1980):168-176.

Irving, L. Homfray. *Officers Of The British Forces In Canada During The War of 1812-15.* Canadian Military Institute, 1908.

Jury, Elsie McLeod. "The Establishments at Penetanguishene: Bastion of the North 1814-1856." *Bulletin of the Museum of Indian Archaeology, University of Western Ontario.* no. 12, 1959.

Jury, Elsie McLeod. "USS Tigress-HMS Confiance, 1813-1831." *Inland Seas.* 28(1972):3-16.

LaJeunesse, E. J. "The First Four Years of the Settlement on the Canadian Side of the Detroit River," *Ontario History.* 47(1955):123-131.

LaJeunesse, E. J. ed. *The Windsor Border Region.* Toronto: University of Toronto Press, 1960.

Lavery, Brian. *The Ship of the Line, Volume II.* London: Naval Institute Press, 1984.

Lossing, Benson J. *The Pictorial Field-book of the War of 1812.* New York: Harper and Brothers, 1868.

Mahan, A. T. *Sea Power In Its Relations to the War of 1812.* 2 volumes. London: Sampson Low, Marston and Company, Ltd., 1905.

Malcomson, R. and T. Malcomson. "The Ship That Didn't Give Up." *Model Ship Builder,* 10(1989):34-37.

Marshall, John. *Marshall's Naval Biography.* Volume 3, Part 1, London: The Admiralty, 1831.

Martin, Tyrone G. *A Most Fortunate Ship: A Narrative History of "Old Ironsides."* Chester, Conn.: The Globe Pequot Press, 1980.

Macpherson, K. R. "List of Vessels Employed on British Naval Service on the Great Lakes, 1755-1875." *Ontario History.* 55(1963):173-179.

Palmer, Michael A. "A Failure of Command, Control, and Communications: Oliver Hazard Perry and the Battle of Lake Erie." *The Journal of Erie Studies.* 17(1988):7-26.

Parsons, Usher. *The Battle of Lake Erie.* Providence, R.I: Rhode Island Historical Society, 1854.

Parsons, Usher. "Brief Sketches of the Officers Who Were in the Battle of Lake Erie." *Inland Seas.* 19(1963):172-189.

BIBLIOGRAPHY

Peckham, Howard H. "Commodore Perry's Captive." *Ohio History*. 72(1963):220-227.

The Perry's Victory Memorial. Souvenir Pamphlet, National Board of Memorial Commissioners, 1913.

Pope, Dudley. *Life in Nelson's Navy*. Annapolis: Naval Institute Press, 1981.

Pratt, Fletcher. *Preble's Boys: Commodore Preble and the Birth of the American Sea Power*. New York: William Sloane, 1950.

Prior, M. D. *The Great Guns of HMS Victory*. Portsmouth: Prior, 1986.

Quinte, Milo Milton, ed. *War on the Detroit*. Chicago: Lakeside, 1940.

Roosevelt, Theodore. *The Naval War of 1812*. Annapolis: Naval Institute Press, 1987.

Rosenburg, Max. *The Building of Perry's Fleet on Lake Erie, 1812-1813*. Harrisburg: The Pennsylvania Historical and Museum Commission, 1987.

Runyan, Timothy J. and Jan M. Copes. "The Battle of Lake Erie After 175 Years: Commemoration and Controversy." *Inland Seas*. 44(1988):264-273.

Severance, Frank H. "What Became of Perry's Fleet." *Buffalo Historical Society Publications*. Vol. 8, (1905): 401-404.

Snodgrass, James M. "A Racing Sailor Looks at the Battle of Lake Erie." *Inland Seas*. 44(1988):132-138.

Spalding, Rufus P. *Oration and Account of the Celebration of the Anniversay of the Battle of Lake Erie*. Sandusky: H. D. Cooke & Co., 1859.

Spurr, John W. "The Royal Navy's Presence in Kingston, Part I: 1813-1836." *Historic Kingston*. 25(1977):63-77.

Spurr, John W. "Sir James Yeo, A Hero on the Lakes." *Historic Kingston*. 30(1981): 30-45.

Stacey, C. P. "Another Look at the Battle of Lake Erie." *Canadian Historical Review*. 39(1958):41-51.

Stanley, George F. G. *The War of 1812—*Land Operations. Toronto: Macmillan of Canada & National Museums of Canada, 1983.

Taylor, William V. "Battle of Lake Erie." *The Perry Victory Centenary*. Ed. George D. Emerson. Albany: Lyon, 1916.

"Testimony in the Court of Enquiry on Captain Elliott Following the Battle of Lake Erie." *Inland Seas*. 40(1984):110-119, 131.

White, David. *The Frigate Diana*. London: Conway Maritime Press, 1987.

Wingfield, David. "Four Years on the Lakes of Canada." Public Archives Canada, MG 24, F-18.

Wood, William C. H. ed. *Select British Documents of the Canadian War of 1812*. Vols. 13-15,17. Toronto: The Champlain Society, 1920-28.

INDEX

41st Regiment 36, 38, 40, 41, 65, 67, 101, 111, 117, 121

Adams, U.S. Brig 15, 61

Aeolus, HMS 23

Albany 45

Alleghany River 47

Almy, Sailing Master Thomas 45, 46, 71

Amelia, U.S. Schooner 51, 70, 71

American Congress 11, 120

American Navy 12, 15, 44

American Revolution 12, 35, 42

Amherst, Lord Jeffrey 35

Amherstburg ix, 13, 17, 31, 32, 33, 34-35, 36, 37, 39, 41, 50, 53, 54, 55, 56, 57, 58, 59, 60, 61, 62, 63, 65, 66, 67, 73, 75, 76, 77, 83, 84, 89, 92, 93, 95, 116, 117, 119, 120, 129

Anson, HMS 20

Ariel, U.S. Schooner 51, 70, 71, 92, 95, 96, 97, 99, 102, 103, 104, 109, 113, 117, 121, 127

Army of the Centre 15

Army of the Northwest 15

Bainbridge, William 71

Barclay, Rev. Peter 20

Barclay, Commander Robert Heriot x, 11, 19, 20-28, 29-36, 39-41, 42, 50, 51, 53-58, 60-63, 64-67, 69-70, 73-77, 83-84, 86-93, 94-98, 101, 102, 111, 113, 114, 116, 117, 118, 119, 120, 121-125, 126, 129

Bass Islands 77, 84, 86, 94, 113

Bathurst, Lord 18, 24

Beaverdams 32

Bell, William 53, 55, 56, 57, 60, 76, 77, 87

Bignell, Lt. George 87, 93, 95, 101

Black Rock 15, 41, 47, 50, 51, 53, 65, 127

Bois Blanc Island 34, 35, 54, 83

Brock, Maj-Gen. Sir Isaac 13, 14, 36, 37, 62

Brooks, Lt. John 100, 113

Brown, Noah 45, 46, 47, 52, 70

Buchan, Lt. Edward 31, 33, 36, 41, 61, 62, 87, 97, 101, 110

Buffalo 15, 46, 50, 69, 71, 122, 123, 127

Burlington 32, 33, 50, 76, 93

Caledonia, U.S. Brig 15, 51, 62, 67, 71, 91, 95, 96, 98, 99, 100, 101, 103, 104, 109, 113

Camden, HMS 56, 60

Campbell, Master's Mate John 97, 110

Cass, Gen. Lewis 118

Centre Division 13, 31, 65, 76

Champlain, Lake 13

Champlin, Sailing Master Stephen 45, 69, 71, 96, 104, 111, 127, 128

Chauncey, Capt. Isaac 14, 15, 17, 18, 19, 30, 31, 32, 44, 45, 50, 51, 69, 71, 72, 77, 82, 120, 123

Chesapeake, U.S. Frigate 92

Chippawa, HM Schooner 33, 39, 56, 65, 87, 92, 95, 97, 99, 100, 103, 104, 109, 110, 113, 117, 127

Clarke, John 97, 113

Clarke, Thomas 101

Conklin, Augustus 71

Constellation, U.S. Frigate 42

Constitution, U.S. Frigate 43, 44, 71, 99

Cossar, Agnes 124

De Rottenberg, Maj-Gen. Francis Baron 14, 65, 66, 67, 73, 75, 117

Dearborn, Maj-Gen. Henry 15, 26, 31, 50, 52, 69

Detroit 37, 51, 62

INDEX

Detroit, Fort 13, 34, 35, 83, 117
Detroit, HMS ix, 11, 54, 56, 57, 58, 60, 61, 65, 73, 75, 76, 77, 78-83, 84, 87, 88, 89, 90, 91, 92, 93, 95-98, 99, 100, 101, 102, 103, 104, 105, 106, 108, 109, 110, 111, 112, 113, 115, 116, 123, 126, 127, 128, 129, 130
Detroit River 12, 13, 34, 35, 54, 61, 67-68, 73, 83, 84, 118, 120
Diana HMS 22
Dobbins, Daniel x, 15, 45, 46, 47, 50, 69, 72, 75, 92
Dover, HMS 86, 93
Duddingstone, Admr. William 20
Duddingstone, Margaret 20
Durham, Capt. Philip 20

Earl of Moira, HMS 17, 26
Eckford, Charles 45, 48, 50, 51
Edinburgh 126
Eighth Regiment 31
Elliott, Commander Jesse x, 15, 45, 70, 71, 86, 89, 92, 95, 97, 98, 103, 104, 105, 109, 110, 111, 114, 117, 118, 120, 123, 125
Erie, Fort 15, 32, 50, 62, 127
Erie, HMS 56, 67, 76, 84, 87
Erie, Lake ix, 11, 13, 15, 19, 30, 31, 32, 33, 34, 41, 44, 45, 46, 51, 52, 53, 55, 62, 63, 65, 66, 70, 74, 75, 76, 77, 85, 92, 110, 112, 116, 117, 120, 124, 125, 127, 130
Erie, town of 40, 41, 45, 46, 47, 50, 51, 64, 66, 71, 73, 82, 113, 116, 123
Evans, Lt-Col. 67

Finnis, Commander Robert 23, 40, 41, 61, 65, 69, 75, 77, 87, 95, 98, 113
Foote, Rr. Admr. Edward James 124
Forrest, Dulaney 71, 99
Forty Mile Creek 33
Frankfort, Kentucky 117
Freer, Noah 26, 63
French Creek 47
Frenchtown, battle of 37-38, 61, 62

Garden, Lt. James 98, 101, 113
Garland, Lt. John 24, 31, 36, 61, 95, 101, 113
General Greene, U.S. Frigate 42

General Hunter, HM Brig 55, 56, 64, 65, 67, 77, 87, 93, 95, 97, 98, 99, 100, 101, 103, 104, 109, 113, 117, 127
George, Fort 31, 50, 67
Gilmor, Robert 60, 61, 63, 76, 77, 83, 93, 123
Gladiator, HMS 124
Grand Island 50, 128
Grant, Alexander 62
Grant, Capt. Charles 22
Gray, Capt. Andrew 17, 26, 32, 60, 62
Guerriere, HMS 44

Halifax 18, 19, 23, 24, 120
Hall, Commander George B. 62, 75, 76, 77
Hamilton, Sec. of Navy Paul 15, 44
Hamilton, U.S. Schooner 77
Harris, Amelia 75
Harrison, Brig-Gen. William Henry 15, 37, 38, 39, 64, 65, 66, 69, 73, 76, 82, 83, 84, 111, 116, 117, 118, 120, 121, 129
Harvey, Lt-Col. John 41, 64
Hennepin, Father 34
Hoffmenster, J. 31, 98
Holdup, Thomas 71
Hull, Isaac 44
Hull, Gen. William 13, 15, 37
Huron, Lake 13, 55, 56, 65, 127

Infernal, HMS 126
Inglis, Lt. George 24, 93, 96, 105, 108, 110
Iphigenia, HMS 23
Irvine, Lt. Robert 62, 98, 115

Java, HMS 71
Java, U.S. Frigate 123, 125
Jay's Treaty 35
John Adams, U.S. Frigate 42, 125
Jones, Sec. of Navy William 44, 45, 51, 67, 82, 83, 114

King's Kettle Fife 20, 23
Kingston 13, 17, 18, 23, 24, 25, 26, 28, 29, 30, 31, 32, 33, 57, 58, 61, 123

L'Achille 22
La Furie 20

148

Lachine 24

Lady Prevost, HM Schooner 33, 34, 35, 36, 39, 54, 57, 62, 64, 65, 67, 77, 83, 87, 90, 95, 96, 97, 99, 100, 101, 103, 104, 108, 109, 110, 112, 113, 117, 127

Laub, Henry 101, 113

Lawrence, Capt. James 52, 92, 95

Lawrence, U.S. Brig 11, 48, 52, 67, 69, 70, 71, 82, 90, 91, 92, 95, 96, 97, 98, 99, 100, 102, 103, 104, 105, 109, 111, 112, 113, 115, 120, 125, 126, 127, 128

Left Division 13

Little Belt, HM Sloop 56, 67, 87, 92, 95, 96, 97, 99, 100, 101, 103, 104, 109, 110, 111, 113, 117, 127

Long Point 33, 40, 41, 61, 65, 66, 67, 69, 70, 71, 73, 74, 75, 76, 83, 92, 93

Lord Liverpool 29

Lower Canada 12

Madison, Pres. James 11, 14, 35, 44

Malden, Fort 35, 37, 55, 59, 64, 66, 76, 83, 86, 89, 92, 117, 120

Mary, Schooner 33, 56

Mary Eliza, Gun Boat 56, 60

Maumee River 37, 38, 39, 56, 77

Mead, Maj-Gen. David 46

Meadville, Pennsylvania 47

Mediterranean 42, 43, 61, 125

Meigs, Fort 38, 69, 73, 76, 77

Miamis, Schooner 56

Michigan Territory 120

Michilimackinac, Fort 56

Middle Sister Island 84, 117

Montreal 12, 13, 30, 118, 123, 126

Moraviantown, battle of 118, 121

Mulcaster, Com. William 30

Myers, Gun Boat 56, 60

Nancy, Schooner 56

Nautilus, U.S. Schooner 42

Nelson, V. Admr. Lord Sir Horatio 22

New Brunswick 24

New York 14, 15, 35, 46, 119

Newark 31, 50

Newport 19, 42, 43, 44, 45, 82, 125

Niagara, Fort 50

Niagara, Peninsula 13, 31-32, 39, 41, 58, 63, 65, 67, 77

Niagara, River 12, 50, 123, 128, 129

Niagara, U.S. Brig ix, 48, 52, 67, 69, 70, 71, 72, 90, 91, 95, 96, 97, 98, 99, 100, 101, 102, 103, 104, 105, 106, 108, 109, 110, 111, 113, 114, 115, 125, 127, 128

O'Keefe, Lt. 73, 74, 111

Ohio, U.S. Schooner 51, 70, 71, 72, 92, 127

Oneida, U.S. Brig 15, 16, 18

Ontario, Lake 15, 16, 17, 18, 26, 45, 67, 69, 72, 75, 77, 93, 118, 120

Packet, Lt. John 71

Parsons, Usher x, 44, 51, 83, 99-101, 102, 111, 115, 128

Perry, Capt. Christopher Raymond 42

Perry, Commandant Oliver Hazard ix, 11, 19, 39, 41, 42-52, 58, 65, 67, 69, 71, 72, 73, 75, 76, 82, 83, 84, 86, 89, 90, 92, 94-99, 102-105, 108, 109, 110, 111, 112, 113, 114, 116, 117, 118, 119, 120, 121, 122, 123, 125, 128

Perry, James 45, 99

Perry Memorial 122, 128

Philadelphia 46, 128

Pittsburgh 46, 47, 58

Point Frederick 25, 26, 27

Porcupine, U.S. Schooner 51, 71, 92, 96, 99, 100, 103, 104, 109, 118, 127

Port Ryerse 33

President, USS 56

Presque Isle 16, 33, 39, 41, 45, 46, 50, 51, 53, 56, 61, 62, 64, 65, 66, 67, 69, 70, 71, 72, 73, 75, 76, 77, 82, 121, 127

Prevost, Sir George 13-14, 17, 18, 24, 26, 29, 30, 32, 38, 57, 61, 63, 65, 67, 77, 83, 118, 123, 126, 127

Prince Regent, HMS 26, 27

Pring, Lt. Daniel 23, 25, 26

Procter, Maj-Gen. Henry 35, 36, 37, 38, 39, 56, 58, 60, 61, 64, 65, 66, 67, 73, 75, 76, 77, 83, 87, 89, 93, 117, 118, 119, 123, 126, 128

Provincial Marine 17, 18, 25, 26, 30, 32, 35, 38, 56, 57, 58, 61, 62, 67, 77, 116, 117, 123
Purvis, Prov. Lt. Francis 95, 102, 124
Put-in-Bay ix, x, 62, 77, 83, 92, 94, 112, 117, 118, 121, 125, 128

Quebec 12, 13, 17, 24, 30, 53, 60, 62, 86, 124
Queen Charlotte, HMS 32, 36, 39, 40, 41, 53, 54, 62, 64, 65, 67, 69, 76, 77, 83, 87, 89, 90, 91, 92, 95-101, 103-110, 112, 113, 115, 116, 125, 126, 127, 128
Queenston 13, 123
Queenston Heights, battle of 14

Ramsgate 22
Redoubtable 22
Revenge, U.S. Schooner 43
Rhode Island 19, 42, 43, 44, 46, 125
Richardson, Robert 116
Right Division 13, 67, 76, 77, 93, 118, 120, 123, 126
Rolette, Prov. Lt. Frederic 33, 61, 62, 101
Rolph, Dr. 75
Royal George, HMS 17, 18, 26, 57
Royal Navy 11, 18, 27, 28, 29, 30, 61, 63, 77, 117, 123
Royal Newfoundland Regiment 67, 75, 89, 101, 117
Ryerse, Capt. Samuel 75

St. Clair, Lake 117, 118
St. Clair River 53, 55
St. Davids 63, 77
St. Lawrence River 12, 15, 24, 30
Sackets Harbour 15, 32, 45, 70, 82, 123
Saint John 24
Saint John River 24
Sandusky 76, 82, 83, 117
Sandwich 35, 56, 89, 117
Schlosser, Fort 50
Scorpion, U.S. Schooner 51, 69, 70, 71, 92, 95, 96, 97, 99, 100, 102, 103, 104, 109, 110, 111, 113, 118, 127
Scourge, U.S. Schooner 16, 77
Senat, George 71
Shannon, HMS 52

Sheaffe, Maj-Gen. Sir Roger Hale 14, 61, 65
Sir Isaac Brock, HMS 26, 27, 57
Somers, U.S. Schooner 51, 71, 92, 96, 99, 100, 103, 104, 109, 110, 113, 127
South Bass Island 112, 113, 121, 122
Southampton, HMS 29
Stokoe, Lt. Thomas 24, 31, 36, 61, 98, 102, 103, 124
Stoney Creek, battle of 41
Strachan, John 20
Swiftsure, HMS 21, 22

Tamasquata, Lake 24
Taylor, Sailing Master William 45, 102, 125
Tecumseh 117, 118
Thames River 83, 117, 118, 120
Tigress, U.S. Schooner 51, 71, 92, 96, 99, 100, 103, 104, 109, 118, 127
Trafalgar 22, 61
Treaty of Ghent 120
Trippe, U.S. Sloop 51, 71, 92, 96, 97, 99, 100, 103, 104, 109, 110, 113, 127
Turkey Point 33
Turner, Daniel 71, 104
Twenty Mile Creek 31
Tyler, John 129

Upper Canada 12, 14, 65, 120

Van Rensselaer, Maj-Gen. Stephen 13
Victory, HMS 21
Vincent, Major General John 32, 41, 64, 65

Warren, Admr. Sir John Borlase 18, 23, 118
Washington 44, 82, 117, 125
Winchester, Brig-Gen. James 37, 38
Wingfield, David 32
Wolfe, HMS 26, 57
Woolsey, Lt. Melancthon 15, 16
Woolwich, HMS 29
Yarnell, Lt. John 98, 100, 102, 104, 115
Yeo, Commodore Sir James Lucas 29, 30, 31, 32, 33, 36, 39, 41, 56, 60, 61, 62, 64, 67, 69, 75, 76, 77, 86, 89, 93, 118, 119, 123, 124, 126, 127
York 13, 26, 27, 30, 31, 57, 58, 59, 76, 77
Young, George 31, 98, 116, 123, 124

PICTURE CREDITS

Introduction
Page 8: Robert Malcomson; Erie County Historical Society.

CHAPTER ONE
Page 13: McCord Museum of Canadian History, Montreal; 14: Metropolitan Toronto Library, J. Ross Robertson Collection (after: MTL/JRR) (T15206); 16: MTL/JRR (T15223); 18: MTL/JRR (T15239).

CHAPTER TWO
Page 21: MTL/JRR (T15258); 23: MTL/JRR (T15259); 24: Public Archives of Canada (C115051); 25: Massey Library, Royal Military College of Canada; 27: MTL/JRR (T15211).

CHAPTER THREE
Page 30: MTL/JRR (T15241); 31: Archives of Ontario (S-1439); 36: MTL (T14508); 37: MTL (T14507); 38, 39: Fort Malden Historical Park, Amherstburg, Ontario; 40: map reproduced from William C. H. Wood, *Select British Documents of the Canadian War of 1812*.

CHAPTER FOUR
Page 43: U.S. Navy Photograph Collection, Erie County Historical Society, Erie, Pennsylvania; 46: reproduced from A. T. Mahan, *Seapower in Its Relations to the War of 1812*; 47: Erie County Historical Society; 48, 49: plans by Melbourne Smith, designer and builder, Pennsylvania Historical Museum Commission.

CHAPTER FIVE
Page 54: Fort Malden Historical Park; 55: Fort Malden Historical Park; 57: National Maritime Museum, Greenwich; 58: painting Margaret Reynolds, detail from *Amherstburg 1813*, Fort Malden Historical Park; 59: Public Archives of Canada (C52252); 62: painting Margaret Reynolds, Fort Malden Historical Park.

CHAPTER SIX
Page 68: painting Peter Rindlisbacher, courtesy of HMS Detroit Project, Amherstburg, Ontario; 70: courtesy of Enoch Pratt Library, United States Naval Institute, Annapolis, Maryland.

CHAPTER SEVEN
Page 74: illustration Owen Staples, reproduced from C. H. J. Snider's *In the Wake of the 1812s*; 78, 79: painting Peter Rindlisbacher, courtesy of Fort Malden Historic Site; 80, 81: painting Peter Rindlisbacher, courtesy of the artist.

PICTURE CREDITS